complete
Puppy
school

complete
Puppy
school

Dr. Quixi Sonntag

NH
NEW
HOLLAND

First published in 2006 by
New Holland Publishers
London • Cape Town • Sydney • Auckland
www.newhollandpublishers.com

86 Edgware Road
London W2 2EA
United Kingdom

66 Gibbes Street
Chatswood
NSW 2067, Australia

80 McKenzie Street
Cape Town 8001
South Africa

218 Lake Road
Northcote, Auckland
New Zealand

ISBN 978 1 84537 173 9 (hardback)
ISBN 978 1 84537 174 6 (softback)

PUBLISHING MANAGERS Claudia dos Santos, Simon Pooley
COMMISSIONING EDITOR Alfred LeMaitre
COPY EDITOR Lizé Lübbe
EDITORIAL ASSISTANCE Nicky Steenkamp
DESIGNER Peter Bosman
PICTURE RESEARCH Karla Kik
PROOFREADER AND INDEXER Rod Baker
PRODUCTION Myrna Collins

REPRODUCTION BY
Resolution Colour (Pty) Ltd, Cape Town
PRINTED AND BOUND BY
Star Standard Industries Pte Ltd, Singapore

2 4 6 8 10 9 7 5 3

Contents

Introduction

Puppies are sweet and loveable, but they turn into big dogs – big dogs that are often uncontrollable and belligerent. Most big dog problems can be prevented if puppies are brought up correctly. This book is for those dog owners who would like to do everything possible to ensure that their puppies become socially acceptable and like-able adult dogs. Its purpose is to empower people to face the challenge of puppy parenting with knowledge and courage. Above all, it should help people understand how to improve the quality of life of the young dogs entrusted to their care.

Choosing the right puppy

The better informed you are when choosing a puppy, the more likely you will be to make the correct choice. But first of all you need to consider why you want a new puppy.

Your choice of a puppy is likely to have a marked influence on your success as a puppy owner. A mismatch between dog and owner can cause the human-dog relationship to turn sour. The better the match between dog and owner (or household), the more likely it is that the relationship will be healthy and lengthy. Although circumstances often favour a hasty, or even emotional decision, it is worthwhile taking time to consider objectively what the best choice of puppy will be for you and your circumstances. After all, taking on a puppy is a 10–15 year commitment and if you make a mistake now it can have serious long-term implications.

If you have already acquired your puppy, this chapter will still be useful, as it will help you in creating realistic expectations of your puppy.

YOUR REASONS FOR WANTING A NEW PUPPY

Critically consider your reason for wanting to acquire a dog. Sometimes what seems to be a perfectly good reason can backfire. If you are getting a puppy for any of the following reasons, it may be wise to reconsider:

The children want a dog

Once a puppy loses its appeal, as it grows bigger, it is quite possible that it may become a burden and a stressor. Contrary to popular belief, puppies and small children do not necessarily combine well. The wrong choice of pet could place unnecessary stress on your household and on an innocent animal. Excitable children can exacerbate puppy boisterousness.

A puppy to help an existing dog with a behavioural problem

You are more likely to end up with two problem dogs. The new puppy is likely to learn from the older dog. Rather first engage the help of a professional to address the problem with the existing pet.

ABOVE *Both children and puppies must learn how to interact appropriately.*

Getting a puppy for security

People often require a dog that is good with children and also a good guard dog. Dogs that are good guard dogs are more inclined to be aggressive to people and children. Although individual dogs in specific circumstances can successfully fulfil this dual role, it is generally not a realistic expectation. Do not expect your dog to be able to distinguish between welcome and unwelcome visitors. Most dogs are naturally vigilant, particularly if they have a close relationship with their owners.

Emotional blackmail

This kind of manipulation can present itself in many ways. Don't allow somebody else's problem with a dog to become yours when you are not ready for it. Don't feel guilty to say no to a puppy as a gift if you are not equipped to accept the responsibility.

Getting a puppy to replace another dog

You cannot expect your new puppy to be a clone of your previous dog, so ensure that you have adequately dealt with the loss before you choose your new pet.

WHAT IT MEANS TO HAVE A PUPPY

Having a puppy means making a commitment. It is not only a time commitment, but also an emotional and financial commitment. It means getting up in the middle of the night for house-training, dealing with puppy chewing, whining and soiling, spending time to train and keep the puppy constructively occupied and spending money. You will need to budget for:

• Buying the puppy
• Veterinary care (routine treatments like deworming, tick and flea control, vaccinations and treatment for when the puppy is sick or injured)
• Medical aid/insurance
• Food

ABOVE *General health care is a lifelong commitment towards your dog.*

• Toys, bedding, collars and leads
• Training classes
• Kennelling when you go on holiday
• Replacement of valuable items destroyed by the puppy
• Public liability insurance

Having a puppy also means enriching your life with a very special companion. The bond between you and your dog could become a very significant relationship for you. To enjoy the full potential of this relationship, you should critically consider your expectations of a puppy.

13

WHAT KIND OF PUPPY WOULD SUIT YOU?

ABOVE *The Afghan hound is an example of a breed that requires high coat maintenance but has a moderately high activity need.*

Your expectations will be influenced by the following factors:

- Your current and future lifestyle
- Type of accommodation
- Family/household composition
- Existing pets
- Your experience as a dog owner
- Availability of resources such as time and money
- Your personality (and that of other members of the household).

Once you have identified the factors that influence your choice, decide which characteristics are important to you:

- Sociability towards people and other dogs
- Activity level
- Sensitive or tough
- Trainability
- Adaptability to various climates
- Susceptibility to heat exhaustion
- Suitability as a first time dog
- Tendency to bark
- Maintenance level with regards to time, financial expenses and coat care
- Watchdog and guarding ability
- Suitability as an outside dog

Use Table 1 (see opposite) to help you identify the dog characteristics that correspond to your expectations. Please note that these are very general guidelines to help you make a good choice – ultimately your personal preference will be the deciding factor.

Table 1

MATCHING OWNER PROFILE TO PUPPY PROFILE

Owner profile		Suitable puppy profile
Lifestyle	• Spend a lot of time at home, work from home	Sociable Sensitive
	• Like to take dog to work/on holidays/on outings	Sociable Easy to train
	• Want a dog to take along when jogging/swimming/hiking	High activity need Not prone to heat exhaustion Sociable
	• Work long hours	Low activity need Independent Low tendency to bark Short coat (low maintenance)
Family composition	• Toddlers and small children; elderly	Not very boisterous Easy to train Sociable
	• Active children	Sociable Tough
	• Allergies in people	Curly-coated dogs are least likely to cause allergies
Accommodation	• Lots of space	High activity need Not necessarily large dog
	• Small garden	Low activity need Not necessarily small dog
	• Apartment	Low activity need Low tendency to bark Easy to train
	• Dog to spend a lot of time outdoors	Heat tolerant in hot climate Cold tolerant in cold climate Independent
Existing pets	• Gender	Opposite gender to existing dog. If more than one dog, the same gender as the least domineering dog.
	• Breed	Both existing dog(s) and new puppy should be sociable with other dogs.
	• Other species	Small animals may be seen as prey, especially by terriers and sight hounds.

15

Owner profile		Suitable puppy profile
Previous dog owning experience	• First time dog owner	Sociable Easy to train Not too sensitive
Available resources	• Have a lot of time	High activity needs
	• Regular grooming not a problem	Long coat Smooth, long coats (i.e. Afghan) require more maintenance than wirehaired coats.
	• Expense not a problem	Rare breeds are expensive. Large dogs cost more to maintain with respect to feeding and veterinary care.
Personality	• Human is an introvert	Dog is sensitive and has a low tendency to bark
	• Human is an extrovert	Dog is tough and independent
	• Human is quite rigid	Dog is independent, not very boisterous and easy to train

ABOVE *Size does matter! These two puppies, a long-haired Dachshund and an Irish Wolfhound, are both eight weeks old.*

MAKING THE RIGHT CHOICE

There are over 400 registered dog breeds world-wide. For practical reasons, we will group and discuss different breeds as breed types. The breed types described in Table 2 are based on the original purpose, or function, of the breeds. The characteristics of each breed type are described and some of the potential physical and behavioural problems are listed. These types do not necessarily represent the groups as used by dog registering and showing authorities.

Table 2

BREED TYPES, CHARACTERISTICS AND BREED EXAMPLES

* = breeds represented in more than one breed type

Breed type	Characteristics	Examples of breeds
Gundogs	• Bred to work in close proximity to people. • Enjoy and need human company, thus very sociable. • Get on well with children, but can be boisterous and knock them over. • Generally get on well with other dogs. • High activity need. • Need space. • Good first time dogs. • Potential problems: Overexcitability, pulling at the lead, destructiveness, hip and elbow dysplasia.	Retrievers, Pointers, Setters, Water Dogs, Standard Poodle, Spaniels, Large Munsterlander, Weimaraner, Hungarian Vizsla, Wire-haired Pointing Griffon, Italian Spinone
Sight hunters	• Bred for hunting by identifying prey by sight, chasing at great speed, capturing and killing. • Independent, used to working alone, somewhat aloof. • Need frequent short spurts of exercise but not be kept constantly on the go. • Can be kept in small space if given enough opportunity to exercise. • Less sociable than gundogs but do get on with people and other dogs. • Suitable first time dogs. • Low tendency for barking. • Potential problems: Difficulty to control off lead due to natural tendency to chase small animals.	Afghan Hound, Borzoi, Saluki, Greyhound, Basenji, Whippet*, Italian Greyhound*, Irish Wolfhound, Deerhound, Lurcher, Ibizan Hound, Pharaoh Hound, Canaan Dog, Rhodesian Ridgeback

Scent hunters	• Bred to use their well-developed sense of smell to track down prey. • Tendency to bark and howl, especially when finding a scent trail. • Work in groups, generally fine with other dogs. • More independent and more sedentary than gundogs. • Strong-willed, can be difficult to train. • Suitable first time dogs. • Potential problems: Long droopy ears require maintenance to keep clean; drooling in some breeds.	Beagle, Bloodhound, Basset Hound, Grand Basset Griffon Vendéen, Petit Basset Griffon Vendéen, Foxhounds, Harrier, Otterhound, Black-and-tan Coonhound, Hamiltonstövare, Dachshund*, Dalmatian
Terriers	• Bred to chase, capture and kill small burrowing mammals. • Tough and robust. • High tendency to bark. • Very high activity need. • Need space. • Excellent watchdogs. • Love physical play, good playmates for energetic children. • Can make very good family pets, but do have a tendency to nip – this needs to be carefully managed. • Potential problems: Aggression toward people and other dogs.	English Fox Terrier, Norwich Terrier, Dachshunds*, Jack Russell Terrier, Norfolk Terrier, Airedale Terrier etc.
Herders and drovers	• Bred to move (herd sheep and goats, and drive cattle) and protect livestock. • Herders are larger and more agile, drovers smaller and stockier (in order to stay clear of the cattle's hooves). • High to very high activity needs. • Sensitive. • Mostly easy to train. • Suitable for experienced dog owners. • Potential problems: Tendency to nip.	German Shepherd Dog*, Belgian Shepherds*, Collies, Sheepdogs, Corgis, Kelpie, Lancashire Heeler, Australian Cattle Dog, Briard, Bouvier des Flandres*, Beauceron, Hungarian Puli
Livestock guarders	• Bred to protect flocks against natural predators. • Large, heavy dogs. • Independent, aloof. Happy to be outdoors. • Cold tolerant. May be prone to heat exhaustion in hot climates. • Moderate to high activity needs. • Not easy to train. • Excellent guard dogs. • Not recommended for the inexperienced owner. • Potential problems: Aggression toward people and other dogs.	Maremma Sheepdog, Anatolian Shepherd Dog, Komondor, Hungarian Kuvasz, Pyrenean Mountain Dog, Estrella Mountain Dog, Bergamasco, Hovawart

Haulers	• Bred for draught work in the colder regions. • Cold tolerant. Happy to be outdoors provided there is adequate social interaction with humans. • High (Siberian Husky) to moderate activity needs. • Fairly independent, can be difficult to train. • Variable sociability. • Potential problems: Tendency to pull on lead. Chow Chow: heat exhaustion.	Alaskan Malamate, Eskimo Dog, Siberian Husky, Bouvier des Flandres*, Bernese Mountain Dog, Great Swiss Mountain Dog, St Bernard, Leonberger, Newfoundland, Spitz-type dogs (Norwegian Elkhound, Spitz, Samoyed, Shiba Inu, Chow Chow*, Keeshond)
Fighters	• Extremely strong jaws; can inflict a lot of damage. • Fighting terriers can be excellent family pets. • Potential problems: Inter-dog aggression, aggression toward unfamiliar people.	Japanese Akita, Shar Pei, English Bull Terrier, Stafford-shire Bull Terrier, American Staffordshire Bull Terrier
Guard and defence dogs	• Originally livestock herders and guarders, or bull- and bear-baiting dogs (dogs used to fight with bulls or bears for entertainment). • Excellent guard dogs. • Can be domineering, need assertive owners. • High (Boxer) to moderate activity need. • Need less space than gundogs, herding dogs and haulers. • Need training. Moderately easy to train. • Preferably an experienced owner. • Bulldog: Very prone to heat exhaustion. • Potential problems: Aggression toward people and other dogs, hip and elbow dysplasia. Boxers: heat exhaustion.	German Shepherd Dog*, Belgian Shepherd*, Rottweiler, Doberman, Schnauzer, Giant Schnauzer, Mastiff, Bullmastiff, Neapolitan Mastiff, French Mastiff, Tibetan Mastiff, Bulldog, Boxer, Great Dane, Boerboel
Companions	• Bred for companionship and comfort (lapdogs). • Many have long but non-shedding coats, ideal for the home, but require regular grooming. • Can be bossy, but usually make excellent family pets. • Thrive on affection from people. • Good first time dogs. • Potential problems: Excessive attention-seeking behaviour, barking, prone to certain orthopaedic conditions, for example, slipping kneecaps, very small breeds with fine build easily fracture legs with rough handling (not ideal for a home with very active children).	Bichon Frise, Cavalier King Charles Spaniel, Chihuahua, Chinese Crested Dog, Havanese, Japanese Chin, King Charles Spaniel, Löwchen, Maltese, Pekingese, Pug, French Bulldog, Lhasa Apso, Miniature Schnauzer, Shih Tzu, Tibetan Spaniel, Mexican Hairless, Toy Poodle, Miniature Poodle, Tibetan Terrier, Bolognese, Coton de Tulear

It is not possible to provide an exhaustive review on dog breeds in this book, therefore the reader is referred to other resources (see Further Resources and Information Sites) for detail.

Don't be surprised if there isn't any breed or breed type that exactly resembles your ideal profile – this is where you'll have to start weighing up pros and cons, taking into account your specific situation and personal preferences.

Knowing what the risk factors are with your chosen breed will enable you to manage these so that they are less likely to become a problem.

Dogs of the same breed are not necessarily the same

When making a choice based on general breed characteristics, keep in mind that, although all puppies from the same breed look more or less the same, they are not necessarily the same in terms of behaviour. While different breeds generally have typical behavioural traits, and breed can to an extent predict the likely behaviour of a dog, there can be differences even within the same breed.

There are two main reasons for this:

- Different breed lines produce different genetic material. Breed lines will differ depending on their use, for example, Border Collies bred to work sheep are quite different to Border Collies bred for the show ring. This explains why breeds in different countries or dogs from different breeders can differ so much in terms of temperament.

ABOVE *In spite of a shared genetic background, littermates often differ from their parents and from each other.*

20

ABOVE *Try to learn more about your preferred dog breed from other owners before you make your final decision.*

• Environmental influences affect a puppy's behavioural development. The inherited genes will determine how a puppy is likely to behave in a given situation. However, the way in which those genetic influences find expression can be influenced by good or bad environmental stimuli. Every experience the puppy has from the moment it is born will affect its ultimate temperament. This is particularly true for the first four months in a puppy's life. What you (and the breeder) do with your puppy has a profound impact on how it will turn out as an adult dog.

Do your own breed survey

Before you can make an informed decision on which breed you would prefer, and considering the potential differences amongst dogs within the same breed, you need to do some practical research. Visit people who own the breeds on

your shortlist – not just breeders, but ordinary dog owners like yourself. Ask them about their perceptions of, and experiences with their dog. Observe how they interact with their dogs and how the dogs respond in various situations, so that you can form a picture of how your short-listed breed may succeed in your own home.

Consider behavioural traits when choosing your puppy

The most common reason for abandonment of young adult dogs is that the owners can no longer cope with some aspect of their behaviour. Behavioural disorders, therefore, are a common cause of death (euthanasia by owner's request) in young adult dogs! Understanding the development of behavioural characteristics and what affects them, and thus forming realistic expectations, is paramount in rearing a puppy successfully.

Environmental influences can affect a dog's temperament

Puppies are born deaf and blind. For the first two weeks they can only use their senses of smell and touch. From about two weeks of age, their eyes and ears open and they begin to experience visual and auditory stimulation. They must be exposed to these stimuli for their eyes and ears to develop normally.

From at least three weeks of age, and even sooner, puppies should receive adequate stimulation in the form of visual and auditory stimuli,

ABOVE *At three weeks of age, puppies can see and hear and start to interact socially with their littermates.*

exposure to different surfaces and textures, as well as handling by, and regular exposure to humans. They should even meet other species such as cats and rabbits as early on as possible. These experiences should all be pleasant but not overwhelming for the puppy. It is thought that puppies are particularly susceptible to the positive effects of appropriate environmental stimulation at three to five weeks of age.

Habituation refers to getting the puppy accustomed to objects and places (see Chapter 3 'The big wide world' for examples), while socialization means getting the puppy used to different types of social interaction with people and other animals. It is the breeder's responsibility to provide appropriate stimulation from three weeks of age or sooner, until the puppies are homed at around eight weeks. Then it becomes your responsibility.

This means actively introducing various visual stimuli (for example, brooms, buckets, refuse bags, umbrellas, bicycles), textures (for example, grass, carpet, tiles, soil) and sounds (made by household appliances, as well as babies crying, alarms, etc.) and frequent, gentle handling by a variety of people.

Puppies that are not adequately exposed to the normal everyday stimuli will be likely to react with fear when they are first exposed to these things at a later stage. Puppies that grow up in deprived environments do not develop the necessary coping skills, have poor learning skills and can develop serious behavioural problems.

ABOVE *Puppies should be gently handled from three weeks of age or younger.*

Early learning experiences

Puppies learn from their own experiences with objects, people and other animals. They learn by association and they also learn by operant conditioning (see Chapter 4), i.e. from the consequences of their actions.

Puppies learn quickly how hard they can bite another puppy before it squeals. They can learn that jumping up against people is rewarding because people reinforce their behaviour with rewards such as petting and attention. The first things that puppies learn are usually the things that stay with them, for example, if a young puppy was taught to sit for treats at a young age, it will tend to sit throughout its life whenever it is unsure of what to do (also referred to as 'default' behaviour). If on the other hand, it has learnt that jumping up is rewarding, this will be its likely default behaviour. Negative experiences early on can have a lasting impact on how a dog's temperament develops later. One traumatic experience as a young puppy can result in a lasting problem.

Inappropriate punishment

Inappropriate punishment of puppies affects their behaviour as adults. Researchers have demonstrated a link between excessive punish-

OPPOSITE Puppies that are exposed to water at an early age are likely to be comfortable with water as adult dogs.

ABOVE *This Irish Wolfhound puppy learns to sit by observing its father.*

ment of puppies during house-training and fear aggression towards people when they are adult dogs. Puppies usually misinterpret punishment as aggression from the person who is punishing them and tend not to make the connection between the punishment and the behaviour that is being punished (see Chapter 4).

The parents' behaviour

Puppies can learn from the example set by their mother or father, particularly the mother. If the mother has acquired a specific fear, for example, the puppies could acquire the same fear. Bitches can affect their puppies' behaviour via genetics as well as learnt behaviour.

ABOVE *By three weeks of age puppies should be exposed to everyday household situations on a regular basis and handled frequently.*

Where to get your puppy

The source of your puppy has a direct impact on its physical and mental development. It has been shown that puppies that come from animal shelters or streetside traders are more likely to develop behavioural and other problems than those that come from responsible breeders or private owners. As noble as it is to take a puppy from a welfare organization, if you are a first-time puppy owner, this is not advised. When you go to view the puppy for the first time (usually from three weeks onwards), observe and ask questions to ascertain the following:

- Is there evidence that puppies are properly exposed to new sights, sounds, smells, textures and human interaction and handling?
- Are the mother and, if possible, the father, on show, of sound temperament (do not bark excessively, show signs of aggression, or shy away from people)?
- Hygienic conditions – clean and not exces-

sively smelly. Fresh water available and easily accessible for the puppies.

- Puppies are in good condition. The mother may look a bit thin and scruffy at around three to six weeks after giving birth, but should not be excessively emaciated, and she should be clean.

- Deworming should take place every two weeks from three weeks of age (including the bitch and all other dogs on the premises).

- The puppies will receive their first vaccination before being sold.

- The breeder is happy to answer all your questions, and also interrogates you. Although it could be a bit disconcerting having a stranger ask you all kinds of personal questions, keep in mind that it is a sign of deep concern over the well-being of the puppies. It is the breeder's responsibility to ensure that his puppies end up well cared for, and you need to give him that assurance. If the breeder seems very eager to sell the puppy without any form of screening, this lack of concern may also indicate other shortcomings.

The best age to home a puppy is around eight weeks. At six weeks, the puppy still has difficulty adapting to the new surroundings. Early weaning and premature removal from the rest of the litter has been associated with a variety of behaviour problems.

TOP *Pets from animal shelters may require special care to rehabilitate them.*

ABOVE *Puppies need social interaction with their mothers and littermates up to around eight weeks of age.*

Male or female?

Males are more likely to urine mark, roam and mount, although these tendencies are mostly controlled with early neutering (see Chapter 8). Females are generally easier to train. They do come on heat every six to ten months but this is eliminated with early spaying (see Chapter 8).

If you already have a dog, it is always better to get a new puppy of the opposite gender. If you have several other dogs, it becomes more difficult to make the right choice. Generally, it is a good idea to choose the gender of the least domineering of your existing dogs. Should you have any dogs with a history of inter-dog aggression, do not get a new puppy.

Making the final choice – choosing the individual puppy

The puppy you choose should be healthy, appear bright and interested and show signs of an even temperament. Spend time with the puppies, observe them carefully and choose a puppy that is middle-of-the-road – not the one that bounds up to you first, but also not the one that huddles shivering in the corner. Don't choose the one that dominates all the others, or the one that is constantly intimidated by its littermates. Choose an even-tempered puppy.

ABOVE *Spend time observing the litter, if possible at various times during the first eight weeks, before you choose your puppy.*

OPPOSITE *Choose a confident puppy from the litter, but not an overactive one or you may have to cope with problems later.*

ABOVE *Training two puppies simultaneously can be challenging. Young dogs tend to focus on each other rather than their handler. However, letting a puppy 'sit in' on a session with its parent or another mature dog can have benefits.*

Getting two new puppies at the same time

This is not very wise for the following reasons: Training one puppy is already time-consuming. However, training two puppies and doing it well is extremely challenging. They tend to focus more on each other than on the handler. If you neglect any aspect of the puppy's upbringing in the first critical weeks and months it can have serious, long-term consequences.

Increased risk for inter-dog aggression: When the puppies reach social maturity at around two years of age (often sooner), there is a high risk of fighting, especially if the two puppies are of the same size (breed) and gender. A responsible breeder will not sell two puppies from the same litter to one person.

The mixed breed puppy

Crossbred dogs can make wonderful pets but the unknown element makes it risky to acquire a mixed breed puppy. The more you know about the mother's identity, her temperament, and how the puppy spent its first few weeks, the more informed your decision will be.

Temperament tests

Temperament tests consist of a series of tests, usually done at seven weeks of age by a person unknown to the puppies. Each puppy's responses are assessed (for example, how it reacts to certain types of handling and to certain environmental stimuli) and accordingly the puppy is described in behavioural terms, such as 'submissive' or 'sociable'.

There are two main problems with temperament tests: firstly, the tests and interpretation of their results are based on unproven theories. Secondly, the predictive value of these tests has not been proven, i.e. if a puppy at the age of seven weeks shows a specific response in a test, does it accurately predict how the puppy will behave in two or three years' time? A comprehensive study showed that there was absolutely no correlation between how the puppies performed during the test and how they ended up as adult dogs. This is most probably due to the huge effect that environmental factors have on the behaviour of dogs.

While temperament tests may be a good indication of a puppy's behaviour at the time the test is performed, it is not useful as a predictor of the puppy's future behaviour.

ABOVE *Find out as much as you can about the origin of a mixed breed puppy.*

2

The puppy's arrival

PREPARATIONS AND INTRODUCTIONS

You have chosen your puppy and will be bringing it home soon. Now it is time to prepare your home and its inhabitants for the puppy.

PUPPY KIT LIST

You will need the following items in order to welcome your new puppy:

Feeding bowl and water bowl(s)

Put a water bowl next to the food bowl as well as in two or three other locations, especially if there are areas where you may temporarily confine the puppy.

Food (that it is already used to)

Find out what the puppy was fed before and ensure that you have a few days' supply of exactly the same food. Sudden changes in the puppy's diet are likely to upset its tummy. If you wish to feed the puppy something other than what it is used to, be sure to introduce the new diet gradually, after a few days.

ACCESSORIES AND BEDDING

Toys should be durable and safe.

Lightweight collar and lead.

Comfortable bedding.

Ensure that the bed is big enough to allow for your puppy's growth.

Bed

Provide a comfortable sleeping place for your puppy. Wicker baskets, enclosed foam beds, mattresses and pillows can be destroyed by puppies. Ensure that the puppy always has alternative chew objects in its bed. A blanket, mat or sheepskin on a few layers of newspaper in a cardboard box is acceptable for a small puppy.

Settle mat

The settle mat could be the same item you use for bedding for your puppy, but must be something that you can easily take with you to different locations. It will be used in training to teach your puppy to lie down quietly at your feet or in another room.

Collar and lead

Use a lightweight collar and lead, for example, nylon or webbing. Chain collars and leads are not suitable for a puppy. They are uncomfortable for the puppy, difficult to handle and a safety risk (see 'Introducing the collar and lead', Chapter 3).

ID tag and/or microchip

To avoid your puppy from being lost, ensure that it is clearly identified. Attach a disc containing your contact details to its collar and also have a microchip implanted.

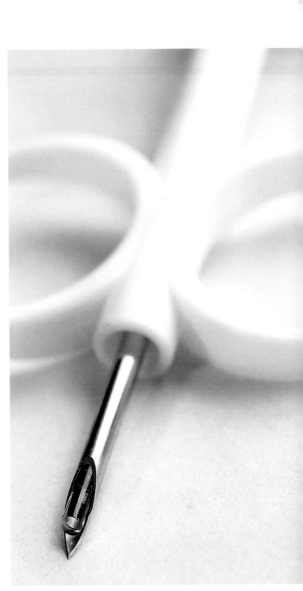

ABOVE *Implanting (injecting) a microchip is a routine veterinary procedure and can be combined with vaccinations.*

Toys

Find a small variety of toys, about three or four. First find out what your puppy enjoys most before you invest in more toys. Ensure that you

35

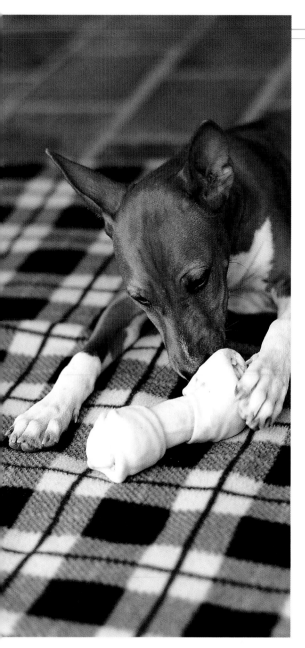

have 'consumable' chew toys such as rawhide chews as well as solid rubber or nylon toys that cannot be easily destroyed. The more expensive toys are often the ones that last longer. Choose safe toys – soft toys are fine for most small breeds, but robust puppies will easily tear a soft toy apart. This poses a health risk as the puppy could ingest parts of the toy, which could lead to intestinal obstructions.

Pee and pooh cleaning kit

Be prepared (both mentally and physically) for cleaning up messes for the first few weeks. Have some paper towelling and cleaning agent ready. The cleaning agent should be a soap that does not contain ammonia. The sooner you can clean up a mess, the better. Commercial odour neutralizers are also useful.

Grooming brush

The sooner you begin grooming your puppy, the sooner it will learn that being handled and groomed is nothing to be afraid of. Puppies have very thin and sensitive skins, so use a type of brush such as the ZoomGroom®, that does not have sharp bristles and cannot hurt. The first grooming experience must be pleasant for the puppy otherwise it will forever have a negative association with grooming.

ABOVE *A rawhide chew toy keeps this Basenji puppy constructively occupied.* TOP RIGHT *The Zoomgroom® is an ideal brush for early introductions to grooming.*

PUPPY-PROOFING THE HOME

As a means to manage your young puppy more effectively, you should be able to control its actions and movements.

Indoor kennels (crates) and playpens

Puppies need to be supervised round the clock. You will not be able to do this for 24 hours every day. Using a safe, comfortable confinement area will not only make it possible for you to get a break from having to constantly watch the puppy, but will also accustom it to being confined for short periods of time. There will always be a time when an older dog will need to be confined temporarily, for example, at the vet, grooming parlour or boarding kennels. Getting used to it as a puppy makes it far less traumatic, and even enjoyable, later on.

You can use an indoor kennel or crate, or a playpen, or both. Ideally, you should have an indoor kennel for confining the puppy at night, and a playpen for daytime. If you use a playpen for a larger breed, ensure that its sides are high enough to prevent the puppy from jumping out.

ABOVE *A safe, portable playpen makes puppy management much easier.*

An indoor kennel or crate should have enough space for the puppy to stand up and turn around, plus the food and water bowls. Puppies grow very fast, so ensure that the crate will be big enough for it when it is several months old.

The most important thing about the use of a kennel or playpen is that the puppy must enjoy being in it. Introduce it to confinement gradually and in a pleasant manner. Do not confine it the very first time you introduce it to the kennel or playpen. Throw some treats inside for the puppy to eat until it enters the pen or kennel voluntarily. Ensure that there are attractive toys for it to play with. Enclose it for just a few seconds at first, gradually building up to a few minutes.

The maximum length of time a puppy should be left confined during the day, after a gradual build-up, is one hour in an indoor kennel and three hours in the playpen. It is, however, a good idea to accustom it to overnight confinement as soon as possible. Ensure that it is confined close by at night so that you can hear when it gets restless and can take it out to eliminate.

Never use this confinement area as punishment – the puppy must always associate it with pleasant experiences. This must become its haven, its place of safety.

RIGHT *Encourage the puppy to enter the indoor kennel voluntarily by placing its food and water bowl inside.*

ABOVE *A baby gate is easily installed and an excellent access management tool for a puppy owner.*

Baby gates

Most puppies are naturally inquisitive and like to use their mouths and teeth to investigate. This often leads to destructive chewing that could set the tone for inappropriate habits in the future. It can also be a safety risk, for example, if the puppy chews electrical cables. Prevention is better than cure: Avoid situations where the puppy can successfully chew on inappropriate objects. Use physical boundaries such as baby gates to prevent it from entering areas that pose risks, for example, the children's bedroom or the formal lounge. It is important to set realistic limits right from the start, as clear boundaries help puppies feel more secure (see Chapter 3).

Preparing the human family

A new puppy will affect everybody in the household, so it is important to include all household members in the preparation for its arrival. It is also important for the puppy to get consistent feedback from all the people in the home so that it may learn quickly and effectively what is expected of it. Discuss amongst each other who will be responsible for the puppy's care and well-being, and how this will be achieved. Anticipate potential problems and decide together how you will deal with them. For the puppy, the most important thing is consistency – everybody must apply the same rules, otherwise it will become confused and unable to learn effectively.

ABOVE *Hold the child's hand in yours with the palm open to discourage nipping.*

Small children, in particular, need to be adequately prepared. They need to learn that:

- Puppies need to rest and cannot be constantly picked up and played with.
- Gentle handling of the puppy is essential – pinching, pulling and poking are not appropriate things to do to a puppy.
- Calm behaviour in children promotes calm behaviour in puppies.
- Puppies should not be disturbed while sleeping or eating.
- When a puppy turns away, hides or growls it must be left alone.

- Feed the puppy treats only when it is calm and controlled, and from an open palm to prevent the nipping of fingers.

ABOVE *Teach your child the correct way of picking up a puppy.*

Preparing the existing pets

It is quite natural to heap lots of love and attention onto a new puppy – it is indeed very difficult to resist this! However, spare a thought for the existing dog or dogs that may perceive the new puppy as a threat to their own well-being.

If you already have pets, it is very important to prepare them adequately for what may, to them, be an intruder. The existing pets should not perceive any loss of privilege because of the arrival of the new puppy. If, for example, the existing dog always used to sleep in the bedroom and is now banished from the bedroom because the puppy is allowed to sleep there, the existing dog will form an immediate negative association with the puppy. The existing dog must not perceive the puppy to enjoy privileges that, in the older dog's view, the puppy has not yet earned. This makes it much more likely for the older dog to act aggressively towards the puppy, whenever the senior dog feels that its access to important resources are threatened.

Do you foresee that your existing pets' movements will be restricted as a result of the new puppy's arrival? Start getting them used to the new rules well before the puppy arrives. Preferably keep the puppy separated from the other pets for the first 24 hours. When you arrive home, always greet the older pets first and the puppy last. Give lavish attention to the other pets in the puppy's presence and reward them for behaving well in its presence by feeding them delicious treats.

If you are unsure of an existing dog's reaction to the puppy, it is safer to keep the dog muzzled during the first introductions. Introduce the muzzle before the puppy's arrival, so that the dog does not associate the muzzle with the new puppy. A muzzle is uncomfortable for most dogs and must be introduced gradually, with the use of food treats to create a positive association.

The first 24 hours

The puppy's move to your home is very likely to be quite traumatic for the little one. Keep the experience as stress-free as possible by not introducing the puppy to the other pets immediately and maintaining the same diet that was fed prior to the move. Prepare a safe place in your home, with the playpen or indoor kennel ready. The puppy will need warmth (such as a hot water bottle) and comfort (something soft).

Immediately upon the puppy's arrival, take it to the location where you would like it to do its business, as it will be likely to need to go. First impressions count – this may save a lot of house-training work later! Once it has eliminated, ensure that it has water and something to eat. Spend as much time as possible with it so that it

OPPOSITE *Ensure that your existing pets get a lot of attention in the new puppy's presence so that there is no chance that they may feel anxious or develop latent aggression or even overt hostility toward the newcomer.*

43

becomes accustomed to you. Take it out to the potty spot to do its business every couple of hours, or as often as you can.

For the first day, try to keep new experiences and social encounters to a minimum.

The first night

As your puppy may feel really lonely the first few nights, make it feel as comfortable as possible. Ensure that it is not too warm or too cold, nor thirsty or hungry. Puppies need frequent small meals. Take it out often to do its business. Keep it close enough to you so that you can hear when it gets restless at night, then take it out to eliminate, but do not fall for the temptation to let it sleep in bed with you – this may become a very difficult habit to break when it has grown into a considerably bigger dog taking up precious space in your bed. You can leave a radio on softly, or put a ticking clock in its bed to keep it company. After the first few nights, you can move the puppy and its bed to the preferred sleeping location.

LEFT *Keep your puppy in its own bed or indoor kennel close to you for the first few nights, like this Miniature Schnauzer.*

INTRODUCTIONS

Humans

Introduce the puppy to one human at a time. Ensure that it is comfortable with the person being introduced before that person handles it. If the puppy resists contact or actively tries to avoid interaction, do not enforce it. Be very patient, and reward calm and relaxed behaviour with treats, praise and games. Outright fear of handling is discussed in Chapter 7 'Shyness' and 'Resistance to handling'.

Existing pets

Once the puppy is settled in, introduce it to your existing pets one at a time. It is worthwhile to take some time doing this correctly, as sudden introductions may have negative long-term consequences. Most of the principles discussed here apply to cats as well as dogs in the household.

Do the introductions on the floor, that is do not pick the puppy up and hold it in your arms. Some older dogs might interpret this as a privilege (occupying a physically higher space) that the puppy is not yet entitled to and they may then react aggressively.

The initial introductions should take place in places that are not of high value to the existing pet or pets. A place of high value would be a place where the older dog spends a lot of time in the owner's presence, or where the owner is perceived to spend a lot of time – this could be the kitchen, or the family room.

ABOVE *Dogs use smell to communicate and familiarize themselves with each other.*

A large physical space will make introductions less tense, while restricted space serves to make dogs feel more threatened. Either do the introductions outside in an area of low value, or in a spacious indoor area where there is plenty of opportunity to 'escape'.

Introduce existing pets to the puppy one by one, starting with the pet that is most likely to accept the newcomer easily. Only once the puppy is fully comfortable with all your other pets should you start combining more than one in a single interaction.

Expose them to each other gradually. This can be done using wire cages or fencing. Keep older

dogs on leads initially; use muzzles if necessary. Head collars (Halti collars – see Chapter 6) are very useful to control dogs without the need for physical force. Be sure to introduce them to the muzzle or head collar before using it in the presence of an unfamiliar pet. Look out for signs of uneasiness such as barking and hair raising in dogs, hissing and tail swishing in cats.

If your dogs enjoy walks, it is a good idea to first introduce them to the puppy during a mutual walk, i.e. while they are having fun. Always do introductions when everyone (people and pets) is calm. Reward appropriate behaviour, both that of the puppy and the older dog. Give them treats for sitting calmly – this encourages relaxation and ensures positive associations with each other.

ABOVE *Unless there is overt aggression, allow existing pets to acquaint themselves with the new puppy.*

Ensure that you do not inadvertently reward tenseness or aggression. If you do see signs of fear or aggression, back off a little (do not reprimand or punish) until the pet relaxes. Then reward it for being relaxed.

Switch roles when you do the introductions – don't always have the same person handling the same pet(s). Still spend 'quality' time (at least 10–15 minutes per day per pet) with each pet each day. Feed their normal daily diet in sight of each other, but not so close that the older dogs become possessive of the food.

3

Puppy management

COPING SKILLS FOR YOU AND YOUR PUPPY

Now that it has settled into its new home, it is time for you to lay the foundation for a long, happy and healthy relationship between you and your dog. This chapter deals with what puppies need in order to get on successfully in the human world, and how you can meet all these needs. Good puppy management skills will make the experience of bringing up a young dog much more rewarding for you.

Structure and consistency

Puppies need structure in their daily lives to help them settle into their new homes and get to know all the rules. Life for young puppies needs to be predictable so that they feel secure. Consistent daily routines can help puppies adjust well to their new home. Feeding and house-training routines should be established immediately. The puppy should also have a play session, training session and exercise session on a daily basis. (How to establish these routines is discussed in detail below.)

Puppies need consistent feedback about their behaviour. If you make rules, stick with them. If puppies know that people and their reactions are predictable, they will be more likely to trust people. Consider how you would like your puppy to behave when it is an adult dog, and

ABOVE *Consistent daily routines like regular walks help puppies to feel more secure.*

begin to reinforce that behaviour right from the start. Do not allow the puppy concessions that you will withdraw as it grows bigger.

Puppies also need consistency in the way that different people deal with them. Dogs are easily confused by inconsistent feedback. Everybody who deals with the puppy should apply exactly the same rules. This includes visitors!

Resource control and leadership

Puppies need to see that people control their resources. This helps to make them feel safe. Resources include food, sleeping place, toys, games and social interaction. In the following pages, we discuss how you can effectively control these resources so that your puppy will perceive you as an effective leader. If they can recognize that people are good resource managers, it takes pressure off them. Puppies that do not perceive people to be good at controlling resources often try to take over control themselves. As they are not equipped to deal with such a responsibility, it usually results in decreased self-confidence, various forms of inappropriate behaviour (for example, excessive attention-seeking behaviour – see Chapter 7) and even anxiety.

Feeding routine

The young puppy still needs small, frequent meals, ideally three to four a day (see Chapter 9). Feed more or less at the same times every day. Start with a feeding ritual right from the start: It

ABOVE *Teach your puppy to sit before you put its food down.*

should learn to sit (Chapter 5) before it is fed, and the bowl should be removed within 10–15 minutes. Many puppies will finish their food far quicker. However, picking up the food bowl within a set time period is a good habit to get into, as this confirms to the puppy, as it gets older, that you control its food resource.

If your puppy is a slow eater, simply pick up the food bowl after a maximum of 20 minutes, even if it hasn't finished eating. Do not fuss, hand feed or add tasty titbits, as this will turn your puppy into a fussy eater. Be matter-of-fact: Eating is a normal function and should not become something the puppy can use to manipulate you.

ABOVE LEFT and RIGHT *Reinforce your provider position by lifting the food bowl just off the floor and feeding a few pellets by hand, or by dipping your hands in the bowl while it is eating.*

On some occasions, you can pick up the food bowl and feed the puppy a few bites by hand. Take the bowl down to floor level and feed from the bowl, so that it gets used to hands in the food bowl. While it is eating, put your hand in the bowl and feed it.

If a puppy that has a poor appetite is also listless, or if the puppy that normally has a ravenous appetite does not eat well for two consecutive meals, it may be sick and needs to be checked by a veterinarian.

House-training routine

Plan your day carefully so that you can take the puppy out to its elimination area or 'potty spot'

shortly after it has awoken, after every meal and after physical activity. The potty spot should be easily accessible for the puppy. It should always be the type of surface that you would like it to eliminate (urinate and defecate) on, for example, grass or soil.

If your puppy will spend most of its time indoors, you may wish to paper-train it (train it to eliminate on paper). However, if you want your puppy to go outdoors to eliminate, it is better to get it used to grass or soil right away.

Puppies usually develop a substrate (surface type) preference at around seven to nine weeks of age. This simply means that they learn to associate a particular type of surface with the act of eliminating, and at this age that association is very strong. If you ensure that your puppy is always on the correct surface when it needs to go, you will be able to house-train it very quickly. It certainly helps if the breeder already started taking the puppies to an appropriate potty spot from three to five weeks of age.

As the act of eliminating is self-reinforcing (we all know the feeling of relief when the bladder or bowel has emptied), puppies can be house-trained without any additional rewards, provided they don't have many opportunities to make mistakes. This requires constant supervision!

You can give the puppy a food treat as a reward for eliminating in the right spot (wait for it to finish first!). If you'd like your puppy to learn to eliminate on instruction, use the treat in conjunction with a word or phrase, for example, 'busy-busy' or 'hurry up'. Say the words while it is busy and give it a treat the instant it has finished. Repeat this often and your puppy will quickly make the connection.

Constant supervision means that you have to be able to watch your puppy all the time – when it starts sniffing and circling, immediately pick it up and put it outside. Do not play with it until it

ABOVE *Ensure that the preferred elimination area is within easy reach for your puppy.*

has done its business. You may even elect to keep it on a lead until it has gone, and only then allow it to play off lead. As it is not always possible to watch the puppy round the clock, make use of the indoor kennel or playpen (see Chapter 2) to confine it for short periods when you are unable to supervise it.

If your puppy has messed inside while you weren't looking, simply clean up the mess without making a fuss. Use soap and water (preferably soap that does not contain ammonia, as this may enhance rather than eliminate the urine smell), and then dry the area thoroughly. You can also use a commercial scent neutralizer to ensure that the residual scent of the urine or faeces does not readily attract the puppy back to that particular spot.

ABOVE *The puppy associates a specific surface such as grass with urinating; this is reinforced through repetition.*

Should you catch your puppy in the act of eliminating in the house or in an unsuitable area, pick it up and take it to the potty spot immediately. Remain neutral and quiet. Reward it with praise and/or a treat when it does its business outside. Do not rub its nose in the mess, or punish it in any other way if it makes a mistake. The puppy does not know any better, and the more often you reinforce the correct behaviour, the sooner it will learn what is required of it. It is your job to ensure that it doesn't get the opportunity to make a mistake.

LEFT *Praise and give a treat as soon as it has finished doing its business.*

The puppy that is punished for messing inside, often learns to do it when people are not around as it associates the punishment with the person who punishes it, rather than with its own behaviour. This could contribute to fear aggression towards people in the older dog. There are several problems with the use of punishment. These are discussed in more detail in Chapter 4.

The secret to house-training is constant supervision, and reward for good behaviour. Most puppies are successfully house-trained within four weeks.

Play routine

Puppies love to play but need to know how to play appropriately, what to play with and how to control themselves during play. Regular play helps a puppy use up its (often excessive) energy. For them, play is an innocent expression of their hunting instincts – that is why they love to chase and catch moving objects (even if that object is a human limb), are excited by squeaky toys (and sometimes squealing children), and like to shred things (like soft toys and pillows).

Puppies need to learn to play according to human rules, which means learning to inhibit that predatory instinct, in particular the biting. The reason puppies tend to chew peoples' arms and legs is because we instinctively move our limbs away, and this encourages the puppy to grab and hold on.

Play regularly with your puppy, but control the intensity of play. As soon as it gets out of control

ABOVE *Encourage your puppy to play with toys rather than human limbs. German Shepherd Dogs have a high activity need. Stop when the game gets rough.*

– either hurting you, vocalising (growling, barking) excessively or getting too boisterous – stop the game. Simply freeze and look the other way. You can even get up and walk away. You must initiate games, and end them, on your terms.

Avoid rough play such as wrestling and uncontrolled chase games. Puppies that are not taught to control themselves in play can become aggressive later on.

Always play with a toy so that your puppy does not become used to playing with human body parts. Dealing with excessive play-biting is discussed in Chapter 7. Teach your puppy to take toys from you without jumping up by having it sit first before it gets its toy. Some dogs love squeaky toys, but if the squeak causes uncontrollable excitability it is better not to play with these.

Tug games have been the topic of controversy: One viewpoint is that tug games can elicit aggressive behaviour in dogs and therefore are not advisable at all. This, in my opinion, is only true if the tug game gets out of control, the dog controls the tug toy and then uses this to control the person with whom it is playing. You can play tug games with your puppy, as long as you can ultimately regain control of the toy with ease. You can tug and let the puppy win, tug and you win alternately until you decide that the game must end. Then you take the toy and put it away. If you cannot do this, it is indeed better not to play tug games with your dog. You can teach your puppy to drop something it has in its mouth (see Chapter 5) – this is handy not only for playing with tug toys, but also if the puppy has something valuable or dangerous in its mouth.

Training routine

Puppies must learn to think before they do something. By incorporating training into the puppy's routine from early on, you will encourage it to think. Training is mental stimulation for a puppy. Chapters 4–6 deal with training in detail.

Start off with five-minute training sessions, so that you retain your puppy's concentration.

OPPOSITE *Teach your puppy to give up the tug toy, initially in return for a treat.*
RIGHT *Puppies enjoy learning new things – expose your puppy to as many new learning opportunities as possible. Training does not have to be limited to traditional obedience exercises. Weimaraners and other gundogs enjoy physical activity.*

ABOVE *Regular running is good exercise, but build up your puppy's fitness gradually.*

Gradually build it up to 10 minutes, one to three times a day. Ensure that the training is always enjoyable and that you end the training session before the fun stops.

Exercise routine

Your puppy needs regular opportunities to get rid of its energy through physical exercise, apart from playing.

As soon as the puppy can walk on a lead, go for regular (preferably daily) walks. While a puppy is growing it is more at risk of injuring joints and growth plates in the bones, so it is important to ensure that exercise is not excessive. It is best to avoid high-impact exercise such as jumping until after it is a year old. Excessive exercise can be particularly damaging to puppies of large and giant breeds, which only complete their growing process at around 18 months of age. Too much high-impact exercise can predispose puppies of these breeds to orthopaedic problems (see Chapter 8).

Walking and controlled running are the best forms of exercise for puppies. Just like human athletes, puppies need to build up their muscles gradually. Start by running short distances and slowly increase the distance as the puppy gets fitter. A daily walk, run or swim (for older puppies) should be part of every dog's life. If you have a very active puppy, you may need to enlist the help of a puppy-sitter or puppy daycare facility to help provide adequate exercise.

Your puppy should be allowed to run off lead only when it is safe to do so (safe from traffic, strange dogs and dangerous objects) and on condition that you can trust it to come when you call it. Where it is safe, let it go off lead but keep its attention focussed on you by playing

ABOVE *Keep a variety of toys in a basket or box, out of the puppy's reach, and hand out different toys every day.*

ABOVE *Make hollow toys more attractive by stuffing them with treats or smearing a little peanut butter inside.*

games like fetch and hide-and-seek (try to incorporate surprises like new toys), to encourage it to keep coming back to you. This teaches it to stay close to you and provides the foundation for a reliable recall.

Toys and chewing

Puppies love chewing things. Provide your puppy with safe toys and ensure that these are more attractive than other potential chew objects in and around your home (for example, electrical cords, furniture and garden irrigation pipes). Smear something tasty (peanut butter, cheese spread, liver pâté) in or on toys. Chew toys and food-dispensing toys are an excellent distraction for the active puppy.

Have a variety of toys and store them in a toy container. It will make things more interesting if you rotate them on a daily or unpredictable basis. Hand some out and put some away, so that the puppy maintains its interest in the toys. If all the toys are available all of the time, it will be more likely to become bored. By controlling the access to toys, you are also reinforcing your role as controller of resources.

Control the puppy's access to rooms that contain expensive furniture or other chewable objects, either by keeping the doors closed or by using baby gates to bar the way. Substances like bitter apple, as well as a variety of commercially available pet repellents, may help make forbidden objects less attractive.

Environmental enrichment

Provide your young puppy with an interesting, stimulating environment that provides ample opportunity for constructive activities, especially when it is alone. Boring environments make puppies look for their own entertainment, which invariably leads to inappropriate behaviour like destructiveness, excessive barking and howling or attempts to escape.

In order to make the environment interesting, there should be many choices available to the puppy. Provide a variety of toys, several different resting areas and various possibilities for physical exercise and mental stimulation.

Appropriate toys, in particular food-dispensing toys, provide excellent stimulation for puppies. Not only do these toys provide something to occupy the puppy's jaws, but they are also mental stimulation for the puppy. The puppy has to figure out how to get the food out – this stimulates thinking (problem-solving). Many of the food-dispensing toys also stimulate physical activity in that the puppy is required to move the toy in order to dispense the food, so it ends up chasing after the toy.

Resting areas are those places in which the puppy chooses to sleep. Dogs often dig a shallow hole in which to lie and it is not always

Dogs have different individual tastes in toys. Experiment with some of the following to find out what your puppy's preferences are:

- Strong rubber toys.
- Different types of rawhide.
- Nylon chew toys.
- Food-dispensing toys.
- The inside of hollow toys can be smeared with a tasty spread or stuffed with treats. On hot days you can freeze it to provide the puppy with a different challenge.
- Tug toys – rope toys, or a piece of cloth tied in a knot. (Tug toys are unsuitable if you cannot retain them after the game.) For entertainment on hotter days you can wet the cloth, wring it out and freeze it.
- Frozen dog biscuits.
- Solid balls.
- Bouncy balls.
- Frisbees (gundogs and collies tend to enjoy these).
- Squeaky toys (these are unsuitable if they cause excessive excitement).
- Soft toys (not suitable for intense chewers).

ABOVE and OPPOSITE *Solving the riddle of a food-dispensing toy, here a Buster Cube®, is mentally and physically stimulating for puppies.*

ABOVE *Whether indoors or out, ensure that your puppy has an interesting view so that it receives enough visual stimulation.*

where we want them to sleep! Refer to Chapter 7 if your puppy is a keen digger. Experiment with different types of bed and bedding and different locations (shady, sunny, enclosed, open, etc.) to determine your puppy's preferences. Dogs prefer to rest close to human activity, for instance in the house where people tend to spend a lot of time or outside where they can see or hear people.

If your puppy spends most of its time outdoors when you are away, place the indoor kennel or playpen outside if possible and provide at least one other comfortable, sheltered resting place. Leave something that has your scent on it with the puppy, for example, a worn T-shirt. Gardens with shrubs to crawl under and different levels

(high and low areas) are more interesting than flat, open gardens. Dogs like to go to the highest point and look out; you may even want to build a structure that your puppy can safely climb onto in order to provide a more interesting view for it to enjoy.

Should your puppy be left indoors when you are away or if you live in an apartment, ensure that there are two or three different sleeping places where it will feel comfortable. The indoor kennel or playpen should always be accessible to it. Also provide a soft pillow, blanket or mat with or without a basket as an alternative resting place. Provide access to a window or door that has a view to provide some visual stimulation.

ABOVE *Teach your puppy to climb up and down ramps and stairs safely.*

Make sure that the puppy can really see out. You may need to provide something safe that it can clamber on to see properly.

If you don't want the puppy on your beds, sofas or chairs, you will need to limit access to the furniture. You can do this by limiting access to a whole room or making the furniture less accessible. You could also place obstacles (for example, chairs) on the furniture to make it impossible for the puppy to jump on.

Interesting smells can be very exciting for a puppy. You can hide or scatter items for it to discover through scent, for example, food pellets, toys stuffed with food, or some old articles of clothing with your scent on them.

For the active puppy, make some equipment it can climb into and onto. You can use traditional agility equipment like tunnels, ramps and drums, or be creative and design your own 'puppy jungle gym'. Just ensure that it is safe for the puppy – no slippery surfaces, not too high and nothing that can entangle its claws.

When you leave your puppy on its own, ensure that the environment you leave it in is completely safe. Puppies can electrocute themselves if they should accidentally chew on electrical cables, and they can easily develop painful intestinal obstructions after swallowing pieces of wood, fabric and other items not intended for ingestion.

some form of interaction (touching, talking, walking, grooming, playing, training, eye contact), giving it that attention when it is not expecting it instead. (See 'Attention-seeking behaviour' in Chapter 7).

Handling and grooming

Ensure that your puppy is handled and groomed on a daily basis. If it gets used to handling early, it will be easy to handle as an adult dog. Let different people handle it. Touch it everywhere on its body, especially the ears, teeth, gums and feet. At first, try not to cover the puppy's eyes with your hand as you handle the muzzle, as this could make it anxious. Rub it on the back, the chest and the tummy. Make this experience pleasant for it by feeding it treats or playing with its favourite toy while it is being handled.

Gently turn the puppy on its back and release it after a tummy tickle. If it wriggles a lot, hold it in that position until it relaxes, then release it. This teaches it that calm behaviour has positive results. If you let it go the moment it starts wriggling, it learns that resisting control gets it what it wants. You should be able to do this without using force. Some puppies wriggle and bite excessively when being handled and need to be desensitized to handling (see Chapter 7).

Controlled interaction with people

One of the most important resources for puppies is attention from people. If they receive unlimited attention on request, they may become excessively demanding of attention. They will also become excessively dependent on attention for emotional well-being, often suffering from anxiety as a result. People need to be seen to control the puppy's access to attention – people should give attention on their terms, and not when the puppy expects or demands it. This implies ignoring the puppy when it insists on

The handling and grooming should take place on the floor as well as on a grooming or examination table. This prepares the puppy for visits to the grooming parlour and the veterinarian. Open the puppy's mouth to look at the teeth, look in the ears and handle the feet often. You can even brush your puppy's teeth.

Even short-coated puppies need to get used to grooming so it is important that the puppy's first experience of being groomed should be enjoyable. Use a brush with soft bristles so that it doesn't cause pain or irritation.

ABOVE *Gently turn the puppy on its back and release it when it relaxes. This teaches your puppy that calm behaviour has its rewards.*

ABOVE *Take your puppy with you as often as possible when you go out.*

The big wide world

Expose your puppy to as many places, people and things as possible but make sure that these experiences are pleasant. Remember, first impressions count! Getting a puppy used to coping with people and other animals is popularly known as socialization. Getting a puppy used to things (objects, places) is referred to as habituation.

Puppies that have many positive exposures to those people and things they are likely to come across later in life have more self-confidence and resilience. Early socialization promotes good social skills, as puppies become used to interacting with people and other pets.

The younger the puppy, the more receptive it is to new experiences and exposure to new stimuli. Puppies should be exposed to as many different stimuli as possible by the time they are 14 weeks old, and from as early as three weeks of age. At around five to six months, puppies

ABOVE *Expose your puppy to many different objects in a pleasant way.*

become less receptive to new stimuli and are more likely to respond with apprehension to something new in the environment.

New stimuli should always be associated with fun, positive things. You can feed your puppy tasty treats, or play with a favourite toy during every new encounter.

Should your puppy be frightened by a new stimulus during these exposures, take it away to have some fun elsewhere, but return later and ensure that it has a positive experience with the stimulus that initially made it fearful. The intensity of the original stimulus may need to be toned down a little at first.

ABOVE *Early exposure to new locations will help your puppy to gain self-confidence.*

67

TOP and ABOVE *These puppies are getting used to everyday things such as appliances and going for rides in a car.*

Here are some suggestions for introducing your puppy to the big wide world:

- Expose the puppy to indoors and outdoors environments.
- Take it with you in the car on short errands, but make sure the window is safely closed.
- Go to the veterinarian when an injection or treatment is not required, and just have fun. Go on fun visits to the grooming parlour and boarding facility.
- As soon as it can walk on a lead, take your puppy with you on walks to explore the big wide world.
- Introduce it to
  - Objects such as the collar and lead, toys, and umbrellas.
  - Different surfaces, for example, shiny floors, sand, sidewalks, and water.
  - Everyday sounds, for example, the vacuum cleaner, washing machine, hair dryer, and trucks.
  - Things with wheels, for example, bicycles, prams, wheelbarrows, and cars.
  - Different people, i.e. babies, toddlers, men, women, people with disabilities, people wearing different garments and accessories, loud people, different races and so on. Parks and flea markets usually have interesting human variations.

Expose the puppy to one or two new stimuli at a time. Do not tire it out with too many new things at once.

Meeting other dogs and animals

It is important that puppies learn how to behave in the presence of other dogs, and even other species. Developing good social skills with other animals helps ensure that your puppy will be safe to take to places where there are other animals, like the veterinary practice and training classes. Learning how to interact with other dogs comes in very handy when the puppy later meets strange dogs.

The sooner it meets other dogs apart from its littermates and mother, the better. Even if you have other dogs at home, your puppy still needs to meet strange dogs in other places. It is important that while it is still small, it has positive interactions with other dogs. Puppies that are attacked by aggressive dogs may never fully recover from such negative interaction.

Don't allow your puppy to play freely with other puppies in the park, or at puppy class. It is not advisable to have puppies playing together uncontrolled as it teaches them that rough play with other dogs is acceptable. The puppies do not learn to inhibit themselves and this makes training them more difficult. In addition, when the puppy grows up and continues to play in puppy-fashion with adult dogs, its play may be interpreted as assertive or threatening behaviour by other dogs, and could result in inter-dog aggression.

All interaction a young puppy has with other dogs should be controlled. However, though 'controlled' does not necessarily mean having them on a lead, initially it is certainly safer to keep both dogs on leads until they appear to be happy with one another.

Have the puppies in a group play one-on-one with each other. While it is very beneficial for puppies to interact with other puppies of similar age, it is also necessary for young puppies to meet adult dogs. The way adult dogs behave is different to how puppies behave, and the puppy needs to understand the difference. Adult dogs may discipline a young puppy by growling at it or pinning it down. This is considered normal and gives the puppy valuable information about overstepping boundaries. It is best not to interfere in such instances. Ideally, these introductions and interactions should take place under the watchful eye of an experienced dog trainer who will know when to intervene and will be able to do so appropriately.

Well-socialized adult dogs will not attack a puppy with the intention to hurt it.

However, some dogs, due to their inherent nature (some breeds are more prone to inter-dog aggression – see Chapter 1) and/or lack of appropriate socialization, may attack a young puppy causing serious injury. This usually happens when the older dog perceives the puppy as a threat. An older dog may feel threatened if a young puppy gains access to a valued resource, for example, food, or a favourite toy, or even attention from the owner.

When you introduce your puppy to adult dogs, ensure that these dogs have good social skills. Introduce it to other species too, such as cats, rabbits and farm animals. If the first introductions are controlled and pleasant, later on it will be more likely to react quite calmly to other animals as an adult dog.

Greeting people

Puppies are genetically programmed to jump and lick their mother's (and other adults') faces as a greeting ritual. We need to reprogramme them so that they learn that acceptable behaviour when greeting humans means keeping all four feet on the ground.

When your puppy is still small, discourage jumping by lowering yourself to greet it. If it does jump, withhold all interaction: Keep quiet, keep your hands to yourself, look away and turn your back on the puppy. Adopt this body language whenever you arrive home too, withholding all interaction until it calms down.

Ask the puppy to sit, or wait for it to offer a sit, and then pay attention to it again. Give it a food or toy reward. Repeat this exercise a few times consecutively, and on a regular basis while it is still young, so that it learns early on that jumping simply doesn't work. Four feet on the ground must always work. Any social interaction with a jumping puppy (even if it is a reprimand – negative attention is still attention) may reinforce the behaviour (see also pages 88–89).

Encourage your visitors to follow the same routine when greeting your puppy. It is usually best to ask visitors not to greet the puppy at all until it either offers good behaviour voluntarily, or, in the case of a very boisterous puppy, until you have it under control on a lead.

Teach good greeting behaviour to your puppy at the front door as well as at the outside gate and boundary fence.

ABOVE *This little girl is following the correct approach by getting down to greet her Labrador Retriever puppy at the puppy's level.*

ABOVE *Introduce new equipment such as collars, leads and harnesses for short periods during mealtimes initially.*

Introducing the collar and lead

Once your puppy is comfortable with a collar and lead, it will be easier to handle and control. Choose a light, comfortable collar made of nylon, webbing or similar material, put it on just before you feed or play with it, and remove it afterwards. After a few days, leave it on for longer until you can leave it on all day.

Once your puppy is used to its collar, you can attach the lead and leave it trailing for short periods of time. Pick it up every now and then, and reward the puppy with a treat or a game if it doesn't pull away from you. Drop the lead if the puppy pulls violently, and first teach it to walk next to you without the lead (see Chapter 6). When it is used to you being at the other end of the lead, start going for regular walks.

Home alone

Your puppy must acquire a certain degree of independence and learn that being alone is not always a bad thing. If it is not exposed to short periods of isolation at this stage, it may never learn to cope with being alone and may develop signs of separation anxiety later on.

Once it accepts its indoor kennel and/or playpen (see Chapter 2), put it in for a few minutes. Return before it becomes agitated and release it – ensuring your departures and arrivals are low key; it mustn't become conditioned to high excitement levels at these times.

Slowly build up the length of time you leave your puppy alone. Some puppies don't have a problem at all being left confined and unattended and will learn very quickly. Others need a very gradual approach to being left alone, and a lot of encouragement, like a favourite chew toy to help them cope on their own.

If your puppy whines when being left alone, you are either doing it too fast, or it has already learnt that whining gets attention. First, reduce the length of time that the puppy is left on its own, before gradually building it up again to longer and longer periods. Anticipate the whining and let it out before it starts to whine. If it starts to whine immediately upon being left alone, you will need to leave it to whine, and the instant it stops whining, go back and let it out of the enclosure.

Once you have ensured that your puppy can cope on its own, you can leave it unattended in an indoor kennel for up to an hour and in the playpen for up to three hours during the day.

ABOVE *If possible, wear your puppy out before leaving it alone so that it will be tired when left on its own.*

73

How puppies learn good manners

To give your puppy the best chance to turn into a well-behaved dog, you need to ensure that it understands what is expected from it in different contexts. First of all, you need to understand why puppies do the things they do, as this will make training your puppy a lot easier. It will help you develop effective canine communication skills to communicate to your puppy what you want it to do. Puppies do not understand human language and cannot communicate verbally the way we do, hence we must learn to communicate in puppy language. Eventually, you will be able to communicate certain instructions verbally to your puppy and it will respond, but there is a learning process that has to be completed first.

PUPPIES DO WHAT WORKS FOR THEM

A puppy will do those things that are rewarding for it. It will try out different things, and those actions that have positive consequences are more likely to be repeated. Puppies are better at learning from the positive consequences of their actions than the negative consequences. This type of learning is referred to as operant conditioning (also known as instrumental conditioning). The positive consequences for certain actions are referred to as positive reinforcement. Puppies can only learn from the immediate consequences of their behaviour. That means that the reward must be there within seconds of the puppy executing the behaviour.

ABOVE *Keep all household items out of reach as they provide positive reinforcement for investigative puppies.*

Catch them doing it right

You should consciously look out for behaviour that you like. It's the little things that count, often things that may seem obvious: the puppy comes when you call it, sits down when you approach it instead of jumping up, chews on a toy instead of your shoe and lies quietly on a mat while you have visitors. Catch it doing something right and reward it!

Rewarding a puppy

Different puppies find different things rewarding. Most puppies love food. You will need lots of tiny, tasty treats to start off with. Initially you will use treats a lot in your training, but as you get to know your puppy better, you will find out what other things motivate it, for example, favourite toys, petting, being let out to chase the birds or riding in the car with you.

Food treats should be no bigger than the size of a pea. Small treats will not interfere with the puppy's normal, healthy diet (see Chapter 9) and will not fill up its tummy so fast that it loses interest in training. Some dogs will work for a portion of their daily food ration, most dogs require something more special to motivate them. Experiment with different treats to see what your puppy likes, and always keep a variety of treats on hand to maintain it interest: cooked chicken (this is the best treat for dogs with sensitive tummies), other types of meat, hot dog sausage, bits of bacon, cheese and biscuits. Cut it into small cubes and keep a supply handy at all times.

ABOVE *This white German Shepherd puppy finds a rope toy highly rewarding.*

Make a list of all the things that your puppy likes, and use these every day to reinforce good behaviour. Play a tug game with it if it lay quietly in its basket while you were eating a meal. Give it a tasty treat for sitting to greet a visitor (good behaviour followed by an immediate positive consequence).

Use environmental rewards: If the puppy waits for you to open the door without scratching or whining, let it run out and chase the birds.

Timing of the reward is crucial – puppies must have immediate feedback in order to learn effectively from the consequences of their actions.

Don't reward unwanted behaviour

Most puppies consider any form of social contact and interaction as highly rewarding. Even negative interaction such as pushing the puppy away or shouting at it could be rewarding for the puppy. Simple eye contact when a puppy is busy doing something naughty may even reinforce the behaviour.

Most nuisance behaviours (jumping up, scratching, whining, excessive barking) are best dealt with by ignoring the behaviour completely. Always remember therefore that any reaction from you could be interpreted by the puppy as reinforcement and exacerbate the problem.

Ignore unwanted behaviour

Ignoring a puppy does not mean that you do nothing. You need to do four things:

- Firstly, break eye contact. Literally look the other way.
- Secondly, keep quiet. Chances are very good that your puppy does not understand a word of what you're saying anyway, so don't waste your breath.
- The third thing to do is to keep your hands to yourself. Make sure you do not touch, shove or grab the puppy.
- Fourth, turn your back and walk away. Be neutral and calm.

ABOVE *This Bulldog puppy must not learn that pawing and jumping up (left) are rewarding. Withhold any form of social interaction until it offers acceptable behaviour – in this case sitting quietly (right).*

This is a useful technique with young puppies that are just beginning with nuisance, attention-seeking behaviours. You will be surprised how often they stop what they're doing when you actively ignore them, to see what you are up to. That presents you with an opportunity to reward the puppy for something positive.

If this method does not have the desired effect, use it in conjunction with interruption.

Interrupt unwanted behaviour

Every time a puppy can successfully complete a behaviour that it has initiated, it will have found it rewarding, and will be more likely to perform that action again in future. The best way to pre-vent this from happening is to interrupt the behaviour so that the puppy is unable to suc-cessfully complete it.

The key to successful interruption is that it must do just that and no more – interrupt the behaviour, without frightening or hurting the puppy. Different things work for different pup-pies. A shake can with a few coins inside gener-ally works very well (see also pages 88–89). However, this could be excessively frightening to a sensitive puppy. A squirt of water from a spray bottle or water pistol is often effective. Add a few drops of citronella oil to the water to make

it less attractive to the puppy that wants to play with the water. State-of-the-art interruption devices are commercially available, for example, an aerosol can that sprays air with a loud hissing sound can be very effective. The interrupter (also known as a distracter) should preferably not be directly associated with you.

The puppy should think that its behaviour is the only thing associated with the interrupter. This is why using your voice is not recommended. The other reason why 'no' doesn't work is that people simply can't sound assertive enough to make an impression on the puppy. If your soft 'no' gradually escalates until you are yelling at the dog, you have in effect desensitized the dog to your voice and it's unlikely to respond. Use what works – a stern 'no' can be effective. For interruption to be successful, it must firstly be applied immediately as the unwanted behaviour is initiated, and secondly, should be used in conjunction with a substitute behaviour. The timing of the interrupter is crucial – if it doesn't happen within seconds of the puppy starting its behaviour, it will not be effective.

Teach a substitute behaviour

We need to focus on what we want the puppy to do, not on what we do not want it to do. By substituting an unwanted action with a preferred or correct one, we are communicating what it is that we expect in a given situation. Constantly telling the puppy what not to do without reinforcing an acceptable substitute behaviour will result in an uninterested puppy that is not keen to learn.

Good substitute behaviours are sitting instead of jumping, coming instead of running away, grabbing a toy instead of grabbing the remote control. Be proactive rather than reactive: Create opportunities for your puppy to do the right things and be rewarded. Chapters 5 and 6 provide more detail on how to train useful behaviours.

The power of anticipation

As you get to know your puppy, you will know which situations are likely to result in problem

LEFT *Teach your puppy that good things follow good behaviour – the Basenji puppy sits before being allowed to take a toy.*

ABOVE LEFT and RIGHT *Always offer an acceptable alternative for unwanted behaviour. Replace the shoe with a toy and keep the shoes away from the puppy.*

behaviour. For example, you may know that it starts whining to be let out at around 6 am. You can pre-empt this by getting up and letting it out before 6 am a few times.

Anticipation and planning can prevent many puppy problems. Rather than making it difficult for your puppy to offer good behaviour, make it easy. House-training is a very good example of how you can make it easy for it to do the right thing by anticipating (that it will need to eliminate after meals, rest and play) and planning (take it to its potty spot at these times).

Puppies learn by association

Puppies are very good at making associations – this is how they learn the meaning of words (they are not born with PhDs in English). If the word 'sit' is repeatedly associated with the action of putting the rump on the ground, the puppy will quickly learn to associate the action of sitting with the word 'sit'. They can also learn unintended associations, for example, if a big black dog attacked a young puppy, it may forever associate black dogs with fear.

Why punishment doesn't work

Most people, when faced with a misbehaving pet, resort to some form of punishment. For the purposes of this discussion, let us define punishment as something scary or painful (to the puppy) used to stop an unwanted behaviour.

There are several problems with punishment. Firstly, while punishment may indicate to the puppy what you do not want (and even this assumption is questionable as you will see when you read on), it gives it no clue about what you do want. Puppies learn best from positive consequences of their actions. Therefore, punishment does not enhance effective learning.

Secondly, as we have already indicated, puppies often misinterpret what we sometimes think constitutes punishment. If we shove a puppy away, shout at it or even just make eye contact, it may find it reinforcing.

Thirdly, and most importantly, even if the puppy experiences punishment as a negative stimulus, it very rarely perceives it as a negative consequence of its own actions. There are four main reasons for this:

LEFT *Anticipate that your puppy will need to eliminate after sleeping, and let it out as soon as it wakes up.*

1. Timing

Punishment can only be effective if it occurs within one second of the puppy initiating the action that is being punished. Even punishing the puppy 'caught in the act' is not going to work if that act has been ongoing for a few minutes, or even a few seconds. Research has shown that in order to be effective, punishment must happen at the very moment the puppy makes the decision to perform the undesired action, not some time later. While this can be achieved in a laboratory set-up, it is very difficult to organize punishment in the normal household to coincide exactly with the behaviour.

2. Intensity

Punishment must be severe enough to make an impression, without causing pain or fear. Scared animals do not learn well. There is a very fine line between abuse and effective punishment. What works for one pet typically does not work for another, and it even varies from situation to situation for the same dog. Even if we did know how each pet and each situation differs, how would we measure the intensity of punishment? It is simply too subjective.

RIGHT *Even fleeting eye contact can be reinforcing. Teach children to turn their heads away from a jumping puppy and keep their hands off it. This is a more effective way of dealing with jumping than any form of punishment.*

83

3. Consistency

For punishment to be effective, it must be applied each and every time the undesired behaviour occurs. Otherwise the dog is successful some of the time and may try even harder to do the undesired behaviour because it receives random reinforcement (successful execution of an action is reinforcing in itself) for that behaviour. Because we cannot always be there to apply punishment when the behaviour occurs, we cannot be consistent, and therefore may exacerbate the problem by only punishing some of the time.

4. Context

Dogs tend to associate punishment with the person applying it, and often other contexts (for example, the location), rather than with their own action. Therefore punishment should preferably occur without being associated with the presence of a person, i.e. remote punishment (and it should occur within one second of initiation of behaviour, every single time, at the right intensity). This is very difficult to achieve in a normal domestic situation.

For punishment to be effective, it has to comply with some pretty difficult criteria, which simply are not realistic given the conditions in which we rear puppies (homes, not laboratories).

LEFT *Dogs are scavengers and puppies will always try to grab a free meal if they can. Don't make it easy for your puppy to steal food!*

ABOVE *The puppy doesn't know that it has done something wrong (made a puddle on the floor). The 'guilty' look is because it can anticipate a negative response from the human, not because it understands that its earlier behaviour was 'wrong' in any way. Puppies can only learn from the immediate consequence of their actions.*

ABOVE *There is no point in scolding or punishing the puppy that did something naughty in your absence. Just clean up the mess and be more vigilant in future.*

Side-effects of punishment

Dogs will not do things that are not to their own advantage. They will not do things that don't work. If a dog has to be repeatedly punished for the same behaviour, the punishment is clearly not effective. The dog is not getting the message. If it did, it would rapidly learn that a given behaviour does not work and will stop doing it (forever.)

A dog that is repeatedly punished does not learn about its own actions – it learns that people are unpredictable and dangerous. This confuses the dog and causes anxiety. A good example is a dog that is routinely punished for being destructive while the owner was out. The dog learns to associate the punishment with the owner's homecoming, the owner's angry body language, and with the remnants of whatever was destroyed in the immediate environment (i.e. it associates the punishment with everything but its own behaviour). It

ABOVE *When a puppy shows submissive body language in the presence of its owner, it is out of fear or respect – much as it would do in the presence of an older dog – not due to guilt.*

attempts to avoid being punished by showing submissive body language (an attempt to avoid conflict) upon the owner's return. The owner interprets this as guilt or an apology (the dog knows it's been naughty) and punishes it. The dog does not know that its actions earlier in the day are the cause of the punishment, it just knows that its owner is about to hurt it.

Eventually the dog may become defensive when it cannot avoid punishment. This leads to aggressive behaviour, and it may eventually attack its owner, or another person, when it feels helpless in any situation that it associates with past punishment. Anxiety and aggression are side-effects of ineffective and inappropriate punishment.

LEFT *Puppies are reinforced for jumping on people because they get attention for it. Negative attention is still attention.*

How to react when your puppy is being naughty

Focus on what you want your puppy to do, not what you don't want it to do. Teach it acceptable new behaviour rather than try to correct unacceptable behaviour.

Step 1

Try to identify any inadvertent reinforcement the puppy may have had for the problem behaviour and withhold such reinforcement (for example, ignore the puppy that jumps up).

Step 2

Teach the puppy an acceptable substitute behaviour (you could teach it to sit for a treat). Then reinforce the alternative behaviour every time it offers it in the context where it would have shown the problem behaviour.

Step 3

If withholding reinforcement for the unwanted action and rewarding a substitute behaviour doesn't work, use an interrupter. Ensure that your timing is spot-on (interrupt the problem behaviour the very instant it occurs), and reward a substitute behaviour.

The ideal learning environment

The ideal learning environment is one in which a puppy is comfortable and relaxed. Puppies that are scared, excited or aggressive are less likely to learn effectively. These emotions could be caused by external environmental stimuli such as strange people and dogs, unfamiliar sounds, sights and smells, and physical pain. There are puppies that are inherently nervous or excitable. Puppies need to learn how to relax before they will be ready for further learning (see 'Relaxation training' in Chapter 6.

Step 4

If interruption and substitution are ineffective, there may be a need that isn't adequately met (see Chapter 3), or an underlying anxiety. If the puppy has a stimulating environment, set routines and reasonable quality time with you, and the problem persists, you may need to call in a professional to identify and address the underlying problem (see Chapter 7).

ABOVE *Withhold positive reinforcement by turning your back and folding your arms (left). If the behaviour persists even when withholding reinforcement, use an interrupter like a shake can (above right). Timing is crucial – get someone to help you.*

RIGHT *Reward substitute behaviour – in this case, standing on all four feet.*

ABOVE LEFT and RIGHT *A puppy lying down on a visual cue. The more elaborate visual cue on the left (body bending forward combined with hand signal) used initially is faded to a more subtle cue on the right (only the hand signal).*

Dogs cannot understand language

Dogs do not have linguistic abilities. They appear to know the meaning of words only because they have learnt through association that certain sounds always accompany certain actions or events. We use words as cues when training because we want the puppy to listen to our verbal instructions.

The cue

This is the signal we use to indicate to the puppy what we want it to do. It could be a verbal command, for example, 'sit' means the dog should sit. Hand signals can also be used as cues in training. Dogs tend to be more visually aware and often follow our body language signals when we think they understand what we tell them. You may, for example, point your finger and lean slightly forward as you say the word 'sit'. When the puppy does sit, it may be doing so because of the body language more than the verbal cue.

Training methods

Dog training is more than just teaching the puppy to respond to specific cues – it is a skill that empowers you to communicate effectively. Communication is a two-way process that involves both parties. Both parties act, and give feedback to each other about each other's actions. Thus, training should enable you to express your requirements more clearly to the puppy, and at the same time should provide the puppy with a channel through which it can communicate its needs to you.

Traditionally dog training focussed on how dogs could perform things that would benefit people. Dogs were forced through coercion, punishment and correction to perform according to people's needs. Nowadays, training emphasizes the need to make the dog a willing, equal participant in the training process. They are trained according to the scientific principles of animal learning, without the need for forceful, harsh methods that cause unnecessary distress to dogs.

With modern dog training methods such as clicker training the dog is encouraged, with the use of food treats and toys, to offer the right behaviour voluntarily and is then rewarded for it. The more it is rewarded for the correct behaviour, the more it offers it. It performs in order to obtain positive consequences, rather than to avoid negative consequences. Its actions are associated with verbal or other cues and it learns to respond to the cues. Accurate, consistent feedback from the trainer about its behaviour tells it exactly what to do to earn rewards. This dog is having much fun training and enjoys the interaction with the trainer. It has a lot of self-confidence and learns to think for itself. This

ABOVE LEFT and RIGHT *A small paw lift is shaped to a 'high five' within minutes by communicating with the puppy using a clicker, without any physical assistance. Clicker training makes use only of positive reinforcement and no physical force.*

When to start training

Start training as soon as possible! The first four months in a puppy's life are critical as this is the time when it is most receptive to learning about its environment. Although older dogs can be taught new tricks, it is much easier to train the young puppy from as early as eight weeks of age. Training from an early age means that puppies are less likely to make mistakes and more likely to learn to do the right things. The first things that puppies learn usually stay with them for the rest of their lives. Early learning is easier, more resilient to unlearning and promotes effective communication between the puppy and people.

How often and how long to train your puppy

You and your puppy should have at least one 10-minute training session every day. The more frequently you can train for short periods the better, for example, four three-minute sessions per day. As your puppy gets older, its concentration span will increase and your sessions can become gradually longer. Very energetic dogs can become over-stimulated, therefore they do better with short, frequent training sessions.

approach to training promotes the dog's mental and physical well-being. What's more, this way of training is highly successful.

The major difference between traditional training (choke chain corrections, punishment) and reward training is that reward training tells the dog what it is doing right so that it can continue doing that (because dogs do what works for them), while traditional training tells it what it is doing wrong (with no obvious indication of what the right thing is).

Keep it fun

Break up the training session into smaller sessions by playing a game in-between the sections of your training session. Always end a session on a high note, and stop while the going is good!

Training tools you will need

Initially all you will need is a supply of tasty treats (see 'Rewarding a puppy' page 75). You will also need a clicker if you choose to train your puppy using clicker training. Clickers are available from pet stores and various Internet sites (see 'Contacts & Information Sites' and 'Further Reading', pages 184 and 186). Carry the treats in a moon bag or special pouch – this makes it easier in the beginning.

Training classes for puppies

Your puppy will benefit from attending puppy school, provided the training methods are purely positive reinforcement and operant conditioning. Beware of schools that advertise 'positive training methods' but in effect use a hybrid of force, punishment and rewards in their training. The best is to ask to attend a few training sessions first, without your puppy , so that you can get an idea of exactly what goes on. If you are refused this request, keep looking for a good puppy school (what have they got to hide?).

ABOVE RIGHT *Play with your puppy during and after training sessions. Attach the clicker to a wristband to make it easier to use.*

ABOVE *Look out for puppy classes where both people and puppies are relaxed.*

The things to look out for in a puppy class are:

- Are the puppies enjoying their training (wagging tails, etc)?
- Are the people enjoying it (smiles, relaxed body language)?
- How many puppies in a class? (Ideally five or six puppies per instructor.)
- What type of restraint is used? (Choke chains are not a good idea; flat collars and head collars are.)
- How are the puppies handled? (Gently – no jerking, pulling, pushing.)
- How are the people treated? (With patience, respect and helpfulness.)
- How are the puppies taught? (Hands-off, luring with treats, as opposed to hands-on, physical force.)
- Is the training area safe?
- Is the training area big enough not to make puppies and people feel crowded?
- Are the puppies allowed to play freely off lead most of the time? (Then it's better to keep looking for a good puppy school – the correct word is 'school', not playground – see Chapter 3 'Meeting other dogs and animals'.)

ABOVE *Two five-month-old German Shepherd Dog puppies meet for the first time.*

• Is it a professional, well-organized set-up? What experience and qualifications do the instructors have? (Any Tom, Dick and Harry can call themselves dog-training instructors.) If you do not have a good puppy school in your area, you can still achieve a lot on your own. Keep reading!

Health risks

You may not find a formal dog training school that will accommodate really young puppies, because there is a perception that puppies are susceptible to diseases before their full course of vaccinations is completed. In my experience, we have trained puppies as young as eight weeks in classes without any problems. As long as all the puppies are vaccinated (anything from 10 days after the initial vaccination with vaccinations kept up to date thereafter), dewormed and healthy and the training facility is clean, it seems to work well. However, it would be wise to discuss this with your veterinarian and local dog schools, as the prevalence of infectious diseases will vary in different geographical areas.

Training is forever

Puppies need the mental stimulation of regular training sessions now and throughout their lives. Even if you can only fit in five minutes on a busy day, it is very important that you try to maintain a daily training routine. If you are unable to join a training club nearby, develop your own training skills through the use of books, videos and Internet resources (see pages 184 and 185).

5

Teaching good manners

THE TECHNIQUE

There are three basic skills that every puppy should learn:

The three W's are:

• Welcome (come when called).

• Wait (stay quietly in one place while other things are happening).

• Walk-along (walk on a lead without pulling ahead or lagging behind).

These are the skills that help puppies cope well in the world of humans, and they are also the skills that help people cope well with puppies. In this chapter the training technique is described in detail using 'sit' behaviour as an example, while Chapter 6 explains how the basic technique can be applied to a range of other behaviours.

ABOVE *Using a treat as a lure to help a puppy perform a roll-over.*

Modern reward training methods like clicker training developed from the basic lure-and-treat concept. In lure-and-treat training, food treats are used to lure the dog to offer certain behaviours, those behaviours are then linked to a verbal or other cue and gradually the food treats are faded out and the dog responds to the cue.

For example, the treat is held in front of the puppy's nose and moved up. The puppy follows the treat, moving its head up and back. The rump automatically drops and it sits. Once the puppy knows the action (will actively sit down expecting a treat), the action is associated with a cue. As the backside hits the floor (not before!), the trainer says 'sit' and the puppy gets to eat the treat. Thus the action of putting the backside on the floor, hearing the word 'sit' and getting a treat are all associated and the puppy quickly learns that it can pre-empt the giving of the treat by sitting down. It also learns the meaning of the word 'sit' and will eventually respond by sitting when it hears that word.

Lure-and-treat training brought a revolution in dog training, but does have certain disadvantages. The main disadvantage is that dogs may become too dependent on the food, which makes it very difficult to eliminate its use.

Another disadvantage of lure-and-treat training is that precision training is difficult, due to the practical difficulty with delivering the reward at exactly the right moment, if, for example, the dog is performing an exercise at a distance away from the handler.

Clicker training is a reward-based training technique that reduces the dependence on food in the training process, and also enables the trainer to identify the split second that the acceptable behaviour is offered without the need to be in close proximity to the puppy, or having food immediately available.

The clicker is a small plastic device that makes a clicking sound. The click is a neutral, distinct sound that always sounds the same. It is paired with the food treat (or other reward) so that the click becomes synonymous with the reward. The click is then used to reinforce correct behaviour. Although food treats are used together with the click, clicker training makes it easier to fade out the use of food, as the click acts as a bridge between the behaviour and the actual reward. The dog thus learns to work for the click, which results in a primary reinforcement (food), rather than just working for food. Clicker training can be used very successfully for precision training,

as the click accurately defines the exact moment the correct behaviour is offered.

Clicker training requires more handler skills than lure and treat training, but can ultimately be taken further, faster, once the handler has mastered the technique.

The click and the treat are both eventually faded out, and ultimately the dog will respond to verbal cues (commands) or hand signals only. To clicker train your puppy, you should start off by introducing your puppy to the clicking sound.

RIGHT *Reward training does not use hands-on or forceful training techniques.*

LEFT *Click first, then treat. Do not anticipate the treat by starting to give the treat before clicking – the dog must listen for the click, not look for the treat.*

metal tab. You can then peel off the strips one by one as your puppy becomes more comfortable with the sound.

We want to associate the sound of the clicker with something really good, so that the click gains significant meaning for the puppy. Do this by clicking once, and immediately give the puppy a treat. Click, and treat, almost simultaneously. Always click first, then treat. Every click must be followed by a treat.

Click and treat many times, in different situations. Your puppy does not have to be doing anything in particular – all you want to achieve at this point, is to show the puppy that the click, which initially had no intrinsic meaning, becomes synonymous with the reward. This way the click becomes meaningful to the puppy.

Conditioning the puppy to the sound of the clicker

A small number of puppies are frightened by the sound of the clicker. First use the clicker at some distance away from your puppy, to test its reaction. Most dogs will just ignore it, or may cock their ears momentarily. If it is scared of the sound, keep it in your pocket to muffle the sound or put a few strips of surgical tape on the

ABOVE *A standard clicker.*

One more thing: Keep quiet! Our natural tendency is to talk to the puppy because we want to tell it what to do. However, your talking means very little to the puppy at this stage – it's like background noise. Talking diminishes the power of the clicker as a communication tool. You will later start using verbal cues, but for now, keep quiet.

ABOVE *Use a variety of small, tasty treats. Soft treats like chicken and cheese are better than dry, hard treats.*

Summary:
- Click first, then treat.
- Follow every click with a treat.
- Keep quiet.

At some point, after a few short sessions, the puppy will realise that 'click' means 'reward'. Now you can start training specific behaviours. Once the puppy has attached meaning to the click, you do not need to repeat the conditioning process ever again. You can start training now!

When to click

From now on, you will use the click to mark specific behaviours. Click at the instant the puppy does the right thing.

The click does not tell the puppy what to do. The click is not used as a cue to indicate what is expected. Use the click to tell the puppy that what it is doing is good. It provides accurate feedback about the puppy's actions, not an instruction to do something. You can use it at exactly the right moment to give the puppy an immediate positive consequence for its action.

To the puppy, the click means the following:
- I did the right thing (event marker)
- I can expect a reward (reward marker)

No click, at this stage, means 'I did not do the right thing, I should try something else'. If the puppy does something wrong, you need not do anything apart from not clicking. No reprimand, no correction, no punishment, nothing. Focus on what it is doing right.

Is a clicker essential?

No, you can train your puppy without using the clicker. Instead of clicking and treating, you can just give a treat. You can do all the exercises described here without the clicker. Try to deliver the treat as quickly as possible so that it occurs almost simultaneously with the behaviour that is being reinforced.

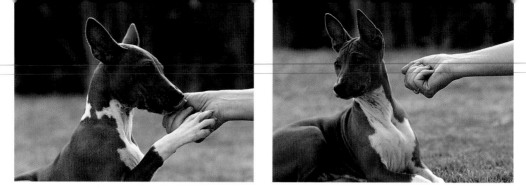

ABOVE LEFT and RIGHT *Keep the treat concealed in your hand for as long as the puppy tries to get at it. When the puppy looks away from the concealed treat, offer it up immediately.*

Puppies that grab treats and bite hands

The short-term solution for nipping is to throw treats on the floor instead of giving it directly to the puppy. However, your puppy will need to learn to take treats nicely. Practise this by concealing the treat in your hand and only releasing it when the puppy stops mouthing or nibbling at your hand. Give treats in your open palm, rather than from your fingertips. An open palm will then become the signal for the puppy that it is allowed to take what is there. Teach children to give treats to puppies with their hands open so that their fingers are not nipped.

What to do if the puppy is not interested in food

Puppies are rarely not interested in food. If your puppy does not show interest in treats, then try to do the following:

- Use better quality treats (from the puppy's point of view). Experiment with different treats - try different types of meat, fish, sweet treats, salty treats, hard treats, and soft treats. Cut them into tiny cubes, no bigger than a pea.

- Ensure that no food is left out for the puppy outside of mealtimes. Pick up its bowl after 15 minutes even if it has not finished eating! If you do not do this, it will think that it controls the food resource (it can go and eat at any time when it is hungry) and that you are not important. If you are the only source of food, it will start appreciating it more.

- Train on an empty stomach, i.e. shortly before the puppy's mealtime.

- A scared dog will not take treats. Ensure that there is nothing in the environment that could frighten the puppy. Start training in a familiar environment, with few distractions.

- Use a toy instead of food. Find out what is your puppy's favourite toy or toys, and use it only during training sessions.

- Use physical interaction and verbal praise instead of food, if it is sufficiently exciting and motivating for the dog.

A STEP BY STEP GUIDE TO REWARD TRAINING

The basic technique of reward training is exactly the same no matter what you are teaching your puppy to do. We will use the 'sit' to explain the process of reward training.

The ability to sit consistently on instruction is in itself a very useful skill for puppies: Dogs that have learnt to sit before receiving any privilege (petting, food, toys and so on) are easier to control and generally less anxious. Sitting is incompatible with most unwanted behaviours – a puppy that is sitting is unlikely to be chewing, barking or chasing at the same time.

The steps in training specific behaviours are:

Step 1: Get (elicit) the behaviour (for example, lure the puppy with a treat)

Step 2: Mark the behaviour (by clicking)

Step 3: Reward the behaviour (give the treat)

Step 4: Fade the food lure (reduce the dependence on the treat as a lure)

Step 5: Name the behaviour (give your instruction a name like 'sit')

If you prefer not to use the clicker, combine steps 2 and 3 in one step.

RIGHT *Start off by teaching your puppy to sit on cue.*

103

GET THE BEHAVIOUR

Luring

Luring means using something that is valuable or interesting to the puppy, usually food, to entice it to do voluntarily whatever we are asking. The idea is that the puppy must offer the behaviour without being forced, so that it works to obtain the reward rather than to avoid correction or punishment. It must think that offering the behaviour was its idea in the first place. This encourages the puppy to figure out for itself what it is that earns it the reward.

This is not bribing. Bribing means giving payment in order to get something done. A reward is payment given in response to a job well done.

Capturing versus luring

Whilst using lures to obtain behaviours is relatively easy, it is quite possible to train most behaviours without lures. The secret is to set up a situation so that the puppy will be highly likely to offer a specific behaviour, and then reward it when it does. This process of rewarding a spontaneously occurring action without luring is referred to as 'capturing' a behaviour. Behaviours that are captured tend to be learnt faster and more reliably than lured behaviours.

Luring the sit

Hold a treat just above the puppy's nose and let it sniff it. Move your hand slightly upwards and

ABOVE *Get the behaviour: let the puppy sniff the treat, as this standard poodle does.*

backwards (away from you, towards the back of the puppy), so that the puppy has to crane its neck in order to follow the scent of the treat.

Problem: puppy jumps up

If the puppy jumps up, you are holding the treat too high. Take it backwards just above its forehead, so that it can keep its front feet on the ground whilst following the treat with its muzzle.

Problem: puppy keeps backing up

If the puppy backs away from you and does not sit, try one of the following approaches:
- Move your hand slower.
- Back the puppy up against a barrier like a wall.
- Construct a tunnel (use chairs or boxes) so that it cannot deviate sideways.

Resist the temptation to push down the puppy's rear end manually – if the puppy thinks it's its own idea to sit, the behaviour will become consistent far quicker and be more reliable in the long term.

ABOVE LEFT and RIGHT *Move the treat up and back so that the puppy moves its head upwards and backwards in order to sit.*

Capturing the sit

You can also capture the sit simply by waiting for the puppy to sit of its own accord, and click and give the treat the instant it does.

Step 2
MARK THE BEHAVIOUR

Watch the puppy's rear end – click as soon as the rump hits the floor. The click must occur within a second of the correct behaviour being offered. (If you were not using a clicker, you would give the treat instead at this moment.)

RIGHT *Here the crate and the wall are used as a tunnel, leaving just enough space for the puppy to sit without moving sideways.*

The importance of good timing

Timing is very important – the click needs to happen at the precise moment that the puppy offers the behaviour. This requires good hand-eye coordination – you should click as you see the rump touch the ground. Focus on getting the timing right. Ask someone to watch you and tell you whether your click coincides exactly with the puppy's action. Practise timing skills by clicking the TV every time your favourite sportsman makes contact with the ball, or ask someone to throw a ball into the air to different heights, and click each time it reaches the top of its arc.

Step 3
REWARD THE BEHAVIOUR

After the click, your puppy must get the treat. The click is after all an event marker as well as a reward marker. Every click is followed by a treat. Always click first, then treat. Repeat the exercise at least six times, and in several training sessions.

ABOVE *Mark the behaviour: click the instant the puppy's rear touches the ground.*

ABOVE *Give the treat.*

ABOVE *You can also throw the treat on the floor so that the puppy has to get up to fetch it. This makes it easier for you to repeat the exercise immediately, as the puppy is already standing.*

Timing the click is more important than timing the treat

Once the puppy knows that the click predicts a treat, it doesn't really matter when the treat comes. If you fumble a bit with the treat, that's fine. Try not to fumble with the clicker! The click enables you to identify the precise moment that the puppy offers the correct behaviour, and it is the click that teaches the puppy that it is doing the right thing.

The click ends the behaviour

After the click, it doesn't matter what the puppy does because the click indicates that it has done the right thing, will be rewarded and that the task is completed. It is not expected to maintain the behaviour while getting the treat.

Quit while the going is good

With time, you will learn how long your puppy's concentration span is and can adjust the number of repetitions per training session accordingly. Refrain from pushing too hard, and always end a session on a high note. Have fun!

Repetition, repetition, repetition

In order to teach your puppy reliably, you will need to repeat the exercise over and over again. Anything that puppies are physically and mentally capable of doing can be trained but needs repetition before the puppy performs spontaneously and accurately. Some behaviours may be well shaped after 10 repetitions, others may require

RIGHT *Fade the lure: the sooner you start using your hand without the lure in it, the better.*

many more repetitions. Repeat at least six times consecutively and train in batches of no more than 20 (stop before your puppy loses interest). Aim for five fluent repetitions of the behaviour in immediate succession, without hesitation from the puppy.

Step 4
FADE THE FOOD LURE

As soon as possible, stop using the treat as a lure, use it as a reward only. This is one of the most critical steps in reward training. You will continue to use food and other rewards generously – but as rewards rather than lures.

Fade the lure by mimicking the exact gesture you used with the lure, except that your hand is now empty. Pretend that you have a lure in your hand, lift it up the same way you did to elicit the sit, click and then produce the reward from your pocket, your other hand or a bowl on the table.

Instead of following the treat in your hand, the puppy will follow your hand. Over time, you can make the hand gestures less obvious.

Fading the food reward (as opposed to fading the food lure) happens much later, once the puppy has made a definite connection between the required action and the cue (see Step 5), and will respond consistently to the cue.

Step 5
NAME THE BEHAVIOUR (ADDING THE CUE)

Once you achieve five smooth repetitions of the sit, you can add the cue. Fluency means:

- Puppy offers behaviour without a food lure.
- The puppy repeats the behaviour without hesitation five times.

ABOVE LEFT and RIGHT *Add the cue: say the word 'sit' as the puppy sits down. With time, the puppy will sit without the prompting hand movement, acting on the verbal cue alone.*

The sequence of events would be as follows:

- Puppy sits (first time).
- You click.
- Puppy gets up to fetch treat (you throw the treat on the floor just in front of the puppy).
- Puppy sits (second time, without hesitation).
- You click.
- Puppy gets up for treat.
- Puppy sits (third time) etc.

To add the cue, say the word 'sit' (or a visual cue like a finger-pointing upwards) just before the puppy sits. The sequence would then be:

- Puppy sits.
- You click.
- Throw treat on the floor so that puppy gets up to fetch it.

- You say 'sit'.
- Puppy sits.
- You click.
- Throw treat, puppy gets up.
- Say 'sit' and so on, until the puppy has sat at least five times in succession.

In effect, you are getting the puppy to offer repetitions of the behaviour while you insert the cue at the appropriate time. After several sessions, the puppy will have made the association between the word (cue) and the action.

Be consistent with the cue

Add the new cue into a few successive training sessions – do not expect the puppy to remember it immediately. Use the cue in exactly the same way every time. Only give the cue once and then wait for the puppy to sit. It is quite normal for puppies to show perfect fluency for a while and then lose it. In ths case, wait patiently, and click immediately when it obeys the command correctly. Avoid the temptation to repeat the cue – your puppy just needs time to think about it. You also don't want your puppy to learn that 'sit-sit-sit' is the cue instead of 'sit'. If the puppy loses focus, get its attention again by moving a few paces or talking to it, then repeat the cue once.

After a few training sessions incorporating adding the cue, the puppy will respond to your cue every time by offering the correct behaviour.

Do not add the cue to two different behaviours in the same training session – this could cause confusion. And bear in mind that dogs have an excellent sense of hearing. It is, therefore, not necessary to shout a verbal cue – whenever you deal with your puppy, be sure to speak in a normal tone of voice.

RIGHT TOP to BOTTOM *Add the cue with fluency by using your empty hand in a luring gesture to encourage the puppy to sit. Be sure to say the word 'sit' and click the moment it puts down its backside. Lastly, throw the treat on the floor for it to pick up from a standing position. Repeat the whole process several times.*

Training in different locations (generalization)

The biggest challenge in dog training is not to teach a particular behaviour, but to maintain a certain level of learning in different environments. Dogs are very context-bound, and are notoriously bad at generalising, i.e. they tend not to apply what they learn in one context easily to a new context.

You are very proud of the new trick you have taught your puppy at home. Now you are at puppy school and want to show off. You confidently say 'Buster, roll over!" and Buster looks at you, as if to say, 'What on earth are you talking about?" You embarrassingly assure the instructor 'But it did it perfectly at home!" The instructor smiles and thinks, 'How many times have I heard that before?"

Buster, in fact, does not know what is expected of it. You have to retrain it in the new environment. It thinks that 'roll over' only applies at home in the back garden. Always start from scratch in a new environment, or an existing environment with new distractions. Each time it will learn faster and learn to generalise quicker.

You should consciously add distractions one by one, and work in different locations, as your training progresses, so that you know that the behaviour you have trained is likely to work properly everywhere, all the time. Start training in a place with minimal distractions, like the bathroom or courtyard. Once the behaviour is at a reasonable level, move to a different location with minimal distractions, such as the dining room. Then move to yet another location, and so on. In every new location, repeat the five steps of teaching the behaviour.

Gradually add distractions (a familiar person some distance away and slowly coming closer, an unfamiliar person far away and approaching, a jogger, another dog etc) in known locations first. Build it up to several distractions in a new location (the park). Every time something changes, go back to basics and retrain from step one. It will become faster and easier the more often you have to retrain in a new environment.

Many dogs are very well-behaved, but only at home. Your puppy needs to behave wherever you take it, and this requires a certain amount of effort that will definitely pay off in the long term.

ABOVE *Once your puppy sits well on cue in a quiet environment, start adding distractions.*

110

ABOVE *The presence of another dog is highly distracting for a puppy. Reward generously for good behaviour in these circumstances.*

Reward more for less in a challenging environment

Make it easy for your puppy to succeed – when the environment makes it difficult for the puppy to perform (for example, many distractions), do not expect the same standard you would expect in an easy environment. Reward the puppy generously for less impressive versions of the behaviour, until you can build it up to the former standard in the new context.

Jackpots

A jackpot is an extraordinary reward, given for extraordinary behaviour. It could be a handful of treats, or something very special that you only give occasionally. Use jackpots for special occasions where your puppy excels either by performing a high standard of a behaviour, or by reaching an important milestone.

Fading the click and treat

Once a behaviour is on cue, you can gradually reduce the use of the clicker and treats. You may click and treat several times for responding to the cue, then ask for the behaviour and reward only with verbal praise or physical interaction. Gradually, use the clicker less and less, until you can phase it out simultaneously with the treat, replacing them with a pat and/or verbal praise.

You should however, not throw your clicker away. Keep stimulating your puppy by training new, fun behaviours like tricks and dance moves, or improve the standard of existing behaviours.

6

Taking training to the next level

Now that you have taught your puppy the first steps of correct behaviour using reward training (Chapter 5), you can hone your skill by training other behaviours. In this chapter we will give you guidelines for training more behaviours. Refer to the five steps described in Chapter 5, as they will apply for each new behaviour you work on. If you don't use a clicker, just give a treat instead of clicking. Very importantly, each new behaviour must be generalised by training in different environments and with a variety of distractions, before gradually fading the click and treat. Please refer to 'Contacts and Information Sites' and 'Further Reading', pages 184 and 185 for detailed references on training.

ABOVE *Train different behaviours, but work in batches. Make small heaps of six to 12 treats to help you keep your batches short and fun.*

Work on several different behaviours in your daily training sessions. Do at least six to 12 consecutive (more as the puppy's concentration improves) repetitions of one behaviour, followed by several repetitions of the next behaviour.

You do not need to cover all the behaviours in one session. You could work on sitting and focus in one session in the morning, and lying down and heelwork in another session later in the day or the next day. Vary the combinations and do not always work in the same sequence – puppies pick up on sequences very rapidly. You need to keep the training sessions interesting and unpredictable so that the puppy will continue to be an enthusiastic learner.

REWARDING THE PUPPY FOR DIFFERENT BEHAVIOURS

Can rewards for different behaviours cause confusion? Maybe your puppy will get confused at first. It will however soon overcome any confusion provided that it gets clear feedback about its actions. If you make it easy for it to offer the correct behaviour, reward it accordingly (click and treat) and repeat the exercise consistently, it will be able to identify what is required. Be patient and do not expect it to do everything perfectly from the start.

It is better not to mix different behaviours in one session, i.e. click for a sit, then a down, then a walk-along when first training your puppy.

ABOVE *Having targeted (touched) the tip of the stick with its muzzle, the puppy looks up in keen anticipation on hearing the click. It is working for the click and understands that this sound will earn it rewards.*

Always work in batches of at least six repetitions of one behaviour. Stick to one behaviour once you have started – do not be tempted to reinforce a perfect down when you have decided that it is a 'sit' batch. Clearly demarcate the end of one batch and the beginning of a new one. You can do this by physically moving to another location, or taking a short break to play a game or just relax with your puppy. You can do several batches in one training session, depending on the puppy's concentration span. Keep the sessions short – no more than 10 minutes at first.

Do not add the cue to more than one new behaviour during one training session. You will find that while you are working on several different behaviours, some will be learnt faster than others. You should only add the cue when the puppy knows what it is doing, i.e. it offers the behaviour almost deliberately, a few times in succession, without being lured, and looks at you as if to say 'So where's my reward?' With some behaviours you will need hundreds of repetitions before you reach this point; in other cases it will happen quickly. Let the puppy lead you in deciding when you are ready to add the cue.

ABOVE *This Weimaraner displays perfect self-coontrol. It is completely relaxed.*

Self-control is the underlying skill that is required for most training exercises, and for everyday coping. In order to perform the three W's (wait, welcome and walk-along) successfully, your puppy requires self-control. It means inhibiting the urge to do something that comes naturally, for example, not chasing the squirrel (but focus on the handler), not grabbing the drumstick (leave it) and not launching at the friendly, frail grandmother (sit and stay). Self-control exercises include the following:

• Focus
• Stay
• Settle down
• Leave

Not only should the puppy learn self-control, but also take it a step further and really relax. The settle down is a good exercise in relaxation.

TEACHING YOUR PUPPY TO LIE DOWN

Luring the down

Lure the puppy into the 'down' position using one or more of the following techniques:

- If the puppy is sitting, use the lure to move its head down, in between its front legs and forward on the ground – similar to an L-shaped movement. Move your hand slowly.
- If the puppy is standing, move its head down and in between its front legs. Hold the treat, concealed in your hand, until it puts its rear end down.
- You could also form a tunnel with your legs, and lure it underneath your legs into a down position. Sit flat on the ground with your knees lifted just high enough for the puppy to be able to fit between your legs and the ground when its chest is on the ground.

Click and treat (C&T) the instant the puppy lies down, in other words the instant the chest and the rump are both flat on the ground.

RIGHT TOP to BOTTOM *Luring the down from the sit: let the puppy sniff the treat and slowly move it down to the ground. Now move your hand forward, horizontally along the ground (middle). Click the instant chest and hindquarters are both on the ground at the same time and give the puppy its well-earned treat.*

LEFT *Use your legs as a tunnel to lure the puppy underneath.*

- It doesn't matter what the puppy is doing when it gets the treat
- Keep quiet!

Fade the lure

Use exactly the same hand movement that you did before, but pretend that you have a treat in your hand. C&T when it lies down. Give the treat with the other hand. Over time, you can use a more abbreviated hand movement.

Add the cue

Once the puppy can lie down five times in succession without hesitation, introduce the cue. Say the word 'down' just before it lies down and C&T. Let it get up to fetch its own treat. Repeat six to 12 times until it makes the connection between the cue and the behaviour.

Capturing the down

Attempt this after your puppy has had a good game to get rid of excess energy. Relax, prepare yourself a drink and observe your puppy carefully. At some point, most puppies flop down if nothing else happens. Capture that moment with a click.

Reminder:

- Every click is followed by a treat
- Click first, then treat
- The click ends the behaviour

TEACHING YOUR PUPPY TO FOCUS ON YOU

Having your puppy's attention is the most important aspect of training. You will not be able to train your puppy in distracting environments if he is unable to focus on you.

This is a good exercise to do when you first enter a new environment. It is the first step in teaching your puppy to walk properly on a lead (heelwork).

Capture the focus

In a familiar environment, sit down and carefully observe your puppy. C&T for attention – just a glance in your direction is good enough. Don't call its name; just capture the spontaneous behaviour of looking at you. Every time it looks at you, C&T. Once you can C&T frequently, start clicking for longer eye contact. Move to other locations and add distractions one by one.

Lure the focus

Sit or stand in front of the puppy and hold a treat in front of its nose. Slowly move it up towards your face. The puppy must follow your hand with its eyes. You can also use a squeaky toy to capture its attention and move that up to your face. C&T when it makes eye contact. Ensure that the puppy is not looking at the food in your hands, but is really making eye contact at the moment you click. You don't want it to learn that looking at food is what is being rewarded. Move your hand away from your face and click while it is still looking at you. Increase the duration by clicking for sustained eye contact.

Add the cue

When your puppy looks at you spontaneously, maintaining eye contact, add a verbal cue like 'look' or even the puppy's name.

ABOVE LEFT to RIGHT *Establish eye contact with the puppy by moving your hand up towards your face and click and treat the moment eye contact is established. Also click and treat for voluntary eye contact when your hand is not luring the puppy (middle). Click and treat for sustained eye contact, i.e. withhold the click for a few seconds while the puppy continues to look at you.*

Relaxation training refers to teaching the puppy to consciously relax itself. It is an essential skill for excitable, boisterous puppies, but all puppies will benefit from it. To teach relaxation you must associate relaxed behaviour with rewards.

Encourage your puppy to settle down on a blanket, pillow or similar item (generally referred to as a 'settle mat'). Do this by ensuring that staying on the settle mat is always attractive for the puppy – that is where it is fed nice treats, given attention and has access to special toys.

Teach your puppy to go to the mat, and relax on the mat. Then you take the mat with you when you take it visiting, and it will be quiet and well behaved on its mat.

First teach the puppy to relax on the mat, and then teach it to go to the mat and finally combine the two behaviours and add a cue.

Relaxation on the settle mat

Put down the mat and sit down on a chair next to it. Wait for the puppy to make itself comfortable on the mat (either sitting or lying down), and immediately click and treat. Concentrate on the puppy's body language. Observe it very carefully and reward any obvious signs of relaxation, for example:

- Slow breathing as opposed to panting.
- A relaxed sit, i.e. sitting asymmetrically, leaning to the side, with the legs outstretched.

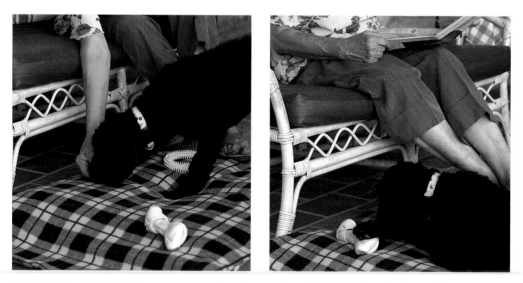

ABOVE LEFT to RIGHT *Wait for your puppy to get onto the settle mat or lure it there with a treat, and get it to settle down next to you. Gradually build up to longer periods of relaxation.*

ABOVE LEFT to RIGHT *Gradually move the mat further away so that the puppy will willingly move away from you to the mat. Click as it reaches the mat, and either toss it a treat or let it fetch the treat from you.*

- A relaxed down - lying with one side of the rump underneath the body, or lying completely on the side with legs stretched out.
- Absence of muscle tension.
- Looking at you rather than staring at things in the environment.

Click initially for tiny signs of relaxation, gradually improving the required standard. Increase the time spent relaxing. Feed it high quality treats without clicking while it is relaxing – you want it to enjoy relaxing, not just look forward to being released by the click. Gradually build up the time spent relaxing (see 'Increase Duration' p130) by reinforcing longer periods of relaxation. Try to build it up to 20 seconds.

Once your puppy relaxes on a settle mat, move it to different locations. Repeat the exercise until it gets used to relaxing in various environments.

Go to the mat and relax

Once relaxed behaviour is associated with being on the mat, regardless of where the mat is, teach it to go to the mat on instruction. Move the mat half a metre away, and C&T every time it approaches the settle mat, then click and treat for actually getting onto the mat, then reinforce lying down or sitting on the mat and finally, reinforce relaxed body language. Move the mat a bit further away and repeat the exercise. Once it will voluntarily go to the mat at about 2 metres, you can add the cue 'settle'.

Adding the cue to long duration behaviour

Always start by adding the cue just before the click. Make sure that you can repeat the exercise fluently a few times before adding the cue. Click for going to the mat and staying there, let the puppy come back to fetch the treat and repeat this five times in succession. Now add the cue as it goes to the mat, click for staying there and let it fetch the treat again.

121

Elicit the recall by calling the puppy and running backwards, away from the puppy. C&T as it arrives. You can also keep it on a lead and reel it in towards you with the lead as you run backwards. Use an excited, high-pitched tone of voice when calling it.

Reinforce casual recalls

Your puppy should always associate coming to you with positive things. Capture recalls when it happens to be coming to you anyway – make these experiences really worth its while by rewarding it with food or attention every time it comes to you. Don't miss out on the normal day-to-day opportunities for reinforcing it. When out walking with your puppy, maintain a high level of interest in yourself by playing games (for example, fetch, hide-and-seek) to encourage it to stay close to you. Keep it on a long lead (or long nylon line attached to its collar) until you feel comfortable about letting it go off lead.

Avoid negative associations with recalls

Never call a puppy to you for a reprimand, no matter what it did before coming to you – it will think that it is being reprimanded for coming to you. (Puppies learn from the immediate consequences of their actions, as we explained in Chapter 4.) If it is misbehaving, go to it and physically remove it from the situation.

TOP *Use friendly body language to encourage your puppy to come to you.*

ABOVE *Note how insecure this puppy looks when approaching a handler who is in an upright posture and leaning forward.*

Your puppy could make a negative connection with the recall, if the recall regularly results in the end of fun. For example, when it is allowed to romp around freely on the beach or in the field and you call it because it's time to go home, it will quickly predict that you are likely to bundle it into the car once it has been recalled. Be unpredictable – recall it a few times, release it again, or go to it, put on the lead and let it go again, or bring it back on a lead when it is time to go.

Use friendly body language

Use friendly body language when calling your puppy. Make it feel welcome by appearing inviting and non-threatening:

- Keep your body low (if necessary crouch or kneel).
- Lean back with your body as it approaches.
- Move back, away from the puppy as it approaches rather than going towards it.
- Some puppies are threatened by outstretched or waving arms.

Reinforce coming as well as staying with you

Encourage your puppy to stay with you after the recall: Every so often, withhold the click until you have the puppy under control and only then C&T. This is to encourage it to stay with you and not just come, grab the treat and rush off again.

Problem: My puppy ignores me when I call it to me.

- If your puppy consistently turns away when you ask it to come, it has probably made a negative association with the cue. Change your cue to something completely different and retrain it. Use a word that does not sound like your previous cue, for example, 'here', 'this way' or even 'shoo', as long as you always use it the same way.
- Set up situations where your puppy will naturally approach you, say the new cue as it

ABOVE *Once your puppy consistently comes to you in a quiet environment, start working in the presence of distractions.*

123

approaches you and reward it generously each time it happens to come. If it comes when you use the new cue, give it a jackpot (see Chapter 5) the first two or three times.

- Your puppy may have entered the 'testing teenager' phase (see Chapter 7) finding everything else much more interesting than you.
- Keep it on a long lead whenever you go out until it is more focussed on you. Ensure that you have exceedingly tasty treats with you. When you call it, gently tug on the lead so that it realises that it has nowhere else to go. Then reel it in towards you, running back-wards and reward it when it is with you. Do not allow it to get away with ignoring you.
- If it is off lead and distracted, surprise it by running in the opposite direction, away from it. It may have learnt to ignore recalls because it has become used to getting a chase game when it doesn't come. Running away will surprise it and make you more interesting than the distraction. As a last resort, lie down flat on your back – this should be sufficiently fascinating for it to come and investigate.
- If your puppy is very shy and will not even approach you, refer to Chapter 7 'Shyness'.

ABOVE *Always make it pleasant for the puppy when it comes to you.*

TEACHING YOUR PUPPY TO WALK ON A LEAD

ABOVE LEFT to RIGHT *Use a treat to encourage your puppy to walk next to you in the heel position without a lead. When it does so consistently, put the lead on but allow it to trail (middle). As soon as your puppy follows, pick up the lead and continue to reward focus.*

See Chapter 3 for tips on how to introduce the puppy to a collar and lead. You can start this exercise off lead, and introduce the lead when your puppy has already learnt to walk next to you without the lead.

For successful walk-alongs, the puppy must learn that being in the 'heel position' is the very best place to be. The heel position is right next to your leg (puppy's head at the level of your knee), left or right, depending on your preference. If your future plans include taking part in competitive obedience, your puppy should always be on your left side. For therapy and for agility dog work, the puppy needs to work on both sides equally well.

The walk-along is taught by building on the focus exercise. Position the puppy next to you in the heel position (sitting or standing), with both of you facing forward, by luring it with a treat.

Reward the puppy for its focus while you remain in a stationary position. Only once you can maintain the puppy in the heel position while standing still for a few seconds, should you start moving forward.

Give one step forward while the puppy is looking at you. If necessary, use a treat in your hand to lure it forward. C&T for every step that the puppy follows you.

Gradually use fewer rewards and C&T for more consecutive steps. Make following you

ABOVE *Start adding distractions as soon as your puppy walks comfortably on the lead (left). A puppy that is allowed to pull on the lead becomes more difficult to control as it grows older (right). Deal with it before the puppy becomes too strong.*

with attention for a few steps highly reinforcing by allowing it to play and sniff and do whatever it enjoys. Then another few steps of walk-along followed by a burst of play and fun.

You can add a cue like the word 'heel'.

The walk belongs to you

Don't follow the puppy where it wants to go. You must be seen to be in charge of the walk. The sooner the puppy learns to follow you, the easier it will be to control it when it is a fully-grown dog. Decide where you want to go and get the puppy to follow you.

Don't pull or drag the puppy. Dragging a hesitant puppy results in increased anxiety. Encourage it with a treat to come back to the heel position. Keep the lead loose – neither you nor the puppy should cause it to tighten. Be patient and don't expect a long, perfect walk immediately. Allow the puppy a reasonable opportunity to sniff and investigate, but don't allow it to pull you around. Use the rewards in the environment to your advantage – let it sniff the tree or chase the birds, but only if it walks there on a loose lead first.

Problem: My puppy pulls on the lead

- If your puppy already pulls on the lead, you need to address the problem immediately. The more often your puppy can successfully pull on the lead and get you to follow, the more difficult it becomes to teach it otherwise.

MAKE THE HEEL POSITION EXTREMELY ATTRACTIVE

Your puppy pulls because the environment provides excellent rewards – new things to investigate. Use really high quality, tasty treats that you would not normally use – your treats have to be more appealing than the environmental rewards! Do this exercise when your puppy is likely to be hungry, and in a location with minimal distractions. Start by standing in one spot, just rewarding being in the heel position. Be prepared for the fact that the first few walks will take you nowhere – just reinforce the puppy for being right there next to you.

INCREASED FREQUENCY OF THE REWARDS

Reinforce the first step before the puppy can get ahead of you. Walk at a fairly brisk pace and C&T continuously as it remains next to you, as often as you can. Ensure that it always gets its treat while it is in the heel position. If you throw the treats ahead of the puppy, it will learn to lunge forward.

TOP RIGHT *Feed tasty treats in the heel position, without moving forward.*
RIGHT *Feed tasty treats every step while moving forward at the same time.*

STOP WHEN THE PULLING STARTS

Stop immediately if the puppy does pull out ahead of you (don't allow pulling to be successful). Freeze the instant it starts pulling, standing squarely on your legs. Then try one of the following strategies:

- Wait for it to look at you – at this moment the lead will slacken. Click as it looks and let it collect the treat in the heel position. Throw the treat just behind you in order to automatically return it to the heel position. Click and treat again immediately while it is still in the heel position. This is the critical point: To reward quickly enough before it gets a new opportunity to pull.

- Change direction and move in the opposite direction the puppy wants to go in. As soon as it is back in the heel position, C&T.

- Move around in a tight circle to get its attention again. C&T as soon as it returns to heel.

USE A HEAD COLLAR

Head collars provide better control over the dog's movements because if you can control the head of the dog, the body will follow. There are different designs available and even special leads to use with them. They are designed not to cause any discomfort or pain, and if used correctly, they can make life with a powerful puller a lot easier. A head collar needs to be introduced

ABOVE *Stop dead in your tracks the instant the puppy pulls forward.*

correctly, otherwise the dog may find it irritating and may constantly try to get rid of it.

The best way to introduce a head collar is as follows:

- Feed the puppy treats from the same hand that is holding the collar.

- Slip the collar over the muzzle while the puppy is eating treats, and then slip it off again.

- Once it is comfortable with this, clip it on at the back behind the ears, but only leave it on for a second or two.

- Repeat this a few times, and then gradually leave it on for longer.

- Put the collar on at mealtimes.
- Attach the lead once the puppy is comfortable with the head collar on its own.
- Some dogs try to get the collar off by rubbing their heads on the ground. Never remove the head collar while the puppy is attempting to get it off. First distract it with a treat or toy, otherwise it learns that struggling will make you take the collar off.

Beware of body harnesses: Some dog harnesses actually encourage pulling, while some specially designed ones will indeed help to keep the dog under control on a walk.

TOP and ABOVE *Introduce the head collar by giving treats while slipping it over the puppy's muzzle, then clip it on behind its ears.*

ABOVE *The head collar provides a humane and effective way of controlling pulling.*

ABOVE *A head collar does not restrict breathing, eating or drinking. The lead is attached to the ring below the chin.*

ABOVE *First increase the duration of the sit by withholding the click (and treat) for longer and longer periods.*

ABOVE *Increase distance by gradually moving away from your puppy. C&T when you are at a distance, or return to your puppy and C&T.*

When your puppy understands the sit and down cues, you can start training the stay. Decide on either a sit or down and stick to that position until the stay concept is well understood. Then it will be easier to apply that learnt skill to another body position. We will use the sit-stay to explain the process.

Teaching stay has two components: Increasing the duration that the puppy is expected to hold this position, while at the same time increasing the distance between puppy and handler. Build each component up separately first.

Increase duration

Ask the puppy to sit and instead of clicking immediately as it performs the action, count silently up to three and then click and treat (withhold the click for a few seconds). Gradually increase the time the puppy remains sitting or lying down. Increase the time randomly so that it has to keep guessing when you will reward it, after three or five or two seconds. If you reinforce in a predictable pattern (three, four, five seconds) it will not try so hard every time.

Increase the time that it holds the sit position without moving away from the puppy until it can reliably sit for 20 seconds.

Increase distance

Once your puppy sits for 20 seconds or longer, you can start moving. First just shift your weight or shuffle your feet and C&T if it did not move. Then give one small step sideways and back again. C&T if it maintains the position. Give a small step to the other side and back. Gradually build up the distance by making the steps slightly bigger and giving two or more steps before you C&T. Again, do not reinforce according to a predictable pattern. When you can safely move about 2m (6ft) away from it, you can systematically start to combine increased duration with increased distance.

Relax the existing standard

When you make tasks more difficult, like moving away during a stay, it is wise to relax previous requirements. Even if your puppy can sit quietly for 20 seconds or more, don't expect a similar performance when you start increasing the distance. And when you work in the presence of distractions relax all previous standards at first.

Once the puppy can hold the sit for 20 seconds at 2m (6ft) , add the cue 'stay'. Ask the puppy to sit, move away and wait for 20 seconds, say 'stay', C&T and return to the puppy. Gradually bring the cue forward (see p121 'Adding the cue to long duration behaviour').

TOP and ABOVE *In the presence of a new distraction, the handler temporarily relaxes the standard, reducing the distance she moves away from the dog. Note the relaxed body language of both puppy and handler.*

131

ABOVE LEFT to RIGHT *Offer the puppy a treat in exchange for the object it is holding in its mouth. Click the instant it opens its mouth to release the object, then give it the treat (middle). The difference between the 'drop' and 'leave' is that with the 'drop' you click for the mouth opening and with the 'leave' you click for looking away from an attractive item (as shown above right).*

Teaching your puppy to drop an item

To teach the drop, offer your puppy a treat or attractive toy in exchange for an item in its mouth and click the instant it opens its mouth. Focus on the opening of the mouth, rather than the item itself, to get the timing right.

Add the cue (for example, 'drop'), and then move on to objects that are more valuable to the puppy, like favourite toys and bones. It is important that the puppy learns to relinquish even very valuable (to it) items when requested to do so. This enhances your role as resource controller, and is an essential skill in the event the puppy holds a harmful object in its mouth. Furthermore, it is the first step in learning how to retrieve (fetch) items.

Teaching your puppy to leave an item

Use the same technique described in Chapter 5 for 'Puppies that grab treats and bite hands'. Show the puppy the treat in your hand, conceal it and wait for the moment it withdraws (maybe in exasperation!) when it realises that the treat is not forthcoming. At that moment, C&T. Reward increasing periods of self-inhibition before adding the cue (for example, 'leave').

The next step is to open your hand gradually so that the treat is partly visible. Say 'leave', wait one or two seconds and click and treat. Gradually increase the time duration. Next, put the treat on the floor and partly cover it with your hand or foot and repeat the exercise. At this stage, it is a good idea to reward the puppy with another treat, not the one on the floor. Perfect the behaviour by gradually moving away so that the puppy will respond to the 'leave' cue even at a distance.

TARGETING

Targeting is the foundation for many useful and more complex behaviours. You teach the puppy to 'touch' certain objects, either with its nose or paw. Then you use that skill to teach a host of other skills. Here's how, starting with nose targeting:

Nose targeting

Use a length of dowel, a ruler or similar object and mark the end of the object with masking tape or paint, so that the tip is easily distinguishable. You can acquire custom-made target sticks from various sources.

The idea is to get the puppy to touch the tip of the stick with its nose. Hold the stick a few centimetres away from its nose and keep it still. It will naturally want to sniff at it. As it moves its nose forward to sniff, C&T. Repeat, until it spontaneously moves forward to touch the tip of the target stick repeatedly.

ABOVE LEFT to RIGHT *C&T first for the puppy looking at the target stick and then for touching it. Hold the clicker and target stick in the same hand and feed treats from the other hand.*

Move the tip of the stick a bit further away from its face, and eventually higher up and low down. Move the stick and see if it will follow the stick – this will deserve a jackpot after the click. Once it offers the behaviour spontaneously and fluently, moving about 30cm (12in) towards the stick, you can add the cue, eg. 'touch'. Give the command just before the puppy touches, click as it touches, and then treat. The sequence is:

- Puppy approaches the stick.
- You say 'touch'.
- Puppy touches the stick.
- Click and treat.

Eventually it will respond to the cue and you will slowly be able to fade out the C&T. Transfer the behaviour to other objects, for example, touching a round lid, a square object or a toy.

ABOVE *Hold the target stick still and wait for the puppy to make its move.*

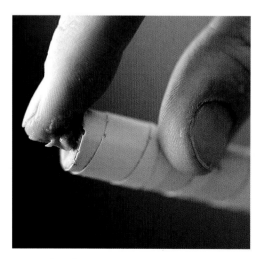

ABOVE *If necessary, you can initially make the tip of the target stick interesting by smearing some peanut butter on it.*

Problem: The puppy is not interested in the stick

- Smear a small amount of peanut butter or another tasty spread on the tip of the stick to make it more attractive and entice the puppy to touch the stick.
- Train on an empty stomach.
- Use a different, more visible target object, for example a stick with a ball on the tip.

Problem: Puppy mouths the stick instead of just touching it

- Click a moment sooner, before it opens its mouth to grab the stick.
- Click only for those attempts that do not include mouthing of the stick.

Uses of nose targeting

Closing doors: Teach your puppy to target a round plastic lid, which you stick to the door at an appropriate height. Ask it to touch it, C&T, then reinforce gradually more forceful touches until it learns to push hard enough to close the door. Make the plastic target smaller and change the cue from 'touch' to 'close the door'.

Changing a cue:

You can change a cue when you have developed a new behaviour from an existing one. The sequence to change a cue is as follows:

- New cue ('close the door').
- Old cue ('touch').
- Puppy closes the door.
- Click and treat.

After several fluent repetitions you can switch to the new cue alone.

Heelwork: Hold the stick just in front of the puppy's nose. Click and treat every step or two that it follows the stick with its nose and continues to walk next to you. Hand targeting (see p136) is also a very effective technique for teaching walk-alongs.

TOP *Use the 'touch' cue and present a new object like a plastic lid.*

ABOVE *Stick the lid to a cupboard door and click when the puppy touches it.*

ABOVE *Teach the puppy to spin around by following the target stick.*

Send away: Push the target stick vertically into the ground and ask puppy to touch the tip. Click and treat. Move half a pace away from the stick with your puppy and repeat. Increase the distance gradually and randomly, until you can send it about 2m (6ft) away. Combine the cue with a hand pointing in the direction of the stick. Add a new requirement by asking it to lie down immediately when it has touched the stick. Shorten the target stick over time, so that the puppy will eventually follow the direction of your hand and lie down when you ask it to, even at a considerable distance.

Tricks: Teach your puppy to 'spin' in a circle, do a figure of eight or 'jump for joy' by following the target stick.

Variations on the theme

Hand targeting: Use your hand as a target object. Start off by holding a treat between your middle and ring finger and let your puppy sniff it, with your hand open. As it sniffs, click and treat. Repeat this only a few times and then hold your hand in exactly the same way, except without a treat. Reinforce any movement of the nose towards your hand. Move your hand so that it follows it and click and treat larger movements towards your hand. Hold your hand next to your side as you walk forward so that it maintains the heel position by continually touching your hand.

Paw targeting: Teach it to target an object like a plastic lid or a ball with its paw. This is an excellent capturing exercise: Put down the object and wait for it to interact with the object, without telling it anything. Even if the paw just moves in the general direction of the lid, C&T. You may have to start off by clicking for it just looking at the object. Once it realises that it is the paw movement that earns it clicks and treats, click for more specific touches, i.e. actually touching the object, and then touching it in the middle with the whole paw. Add the cue (for example, 'paw'). This skill is useful for later agility training when the puppy has to learn to touch the contact zones of obstacles among other things.

Give a paw

Show the puppy the treat in your hand and then conceal it in your fist and let it sniff your hand. It will try to get to the treat with its muzzle first and if that does not work, most puppies try using their paw. C&T when it paws at your hand. Next, use your fist without the treat in it, and add the cue 'say hello' or 'give paw'. You can refine this trick by differentiating between left and right with different cues, and developing it into a 'high five' (reinforce higher paw movements) and wave (multiple paw movements).

Roll over

In the down position, wait for the puppy to assume a relaxed position with the one hip asymmetrically underneath the body. Use a food treat to lure its head so that the neck bends sideways first until it faces backwards and eventually flops onto its side, over on its back and onto the opposite side.

TOP LEFT to RIGHT and ABOVE *To teach your puppy to 'give paw' click even the slightest paw movement at first and treat. Initially, it is fine to click any movement of either paw (middle). Eventually, you click only for paw movement directly onto your hand.*

7

Dealing with behavioural problems

Certain things need to be in place to ensure that your puppy has a good start and the best possible opportunity to become a well-adjusted and obedient companion rather than an annoying dog with one or more behaviour problems. How to provide for the puppy's basic needs is described in Chapter 3. This chapter takes a look at common behaviour problems and offers practical advice and ways of dealing with them.

Back to basics

For the puppy that already has a behaviour problem, you need to revisit these needs and ensure that they are adequately addressed before you focus on the problem behaviour itself. In many instances, just correcting the basics already brings about a noticeable improvement.

- Refer in particular to the following sections in Chapter 3:
- Structure and consistency
- Feeding routine
- Training routine
- Exercise routine
- Toys and chewing
- Environmental enrichment: Choices
- Controlled interaction with people

Review the principles of teaching appropriate behaviour in Chapter 4 ('How to react when your puppy is being naughty').

Be realistic about what you expect when working to correct problem behaviour – set smaller, obtainable goals first and then gradually build it up to more difficult levels.

Identify triggers for problem behaviour

What immediately precedes a puppy's misbehaviour? Can you directly link anything in the environment to the puppy's problem? If you can identify triggers, try to address them as follows:

ABOVE *If your dog is aggressive, prevent situations that will aggravate it.*

- Eliminate the trigger: This is where common sense management is often required. For example, maybe your puppy barks non-stop at the neighbours' cat on the wall. Negotiate a time-share system with your neighbours, whereby they agree to keep their cat in at certain times and you confine your puppy at others. If the puppy insists on grabbing the washing off the line, maybe you should consider setting up a washing line where the puppy will not have access to it. Often, just simple common sense planning may be more successful than complicated behavioural modification techniques.

- Change the puppy's response to the trigger: It may not be possible to remove a trigger altogether. Teach the puppy to change the way it feels about and reacts to the stimulus that causes the problem behaviour. This process is called desensitization and counterconditioning. Problems that are likely to respond well to this approach include puppies that are resistant to handling, shy to interact with people, fearful of things in the

environment, aggressive to people and/or other animals and prone to overexcitement.

Desensitization and counterconditioning

Desensitization (the correct term is systematic desensitization) is a controlled process of gradual exposure to a negative stimulus to get the puppy used to the stimulus. The puppy is first exposed to a mild version of the stimulus, i.e. the stimulus is at a level that does not elicit the inappropriate response such as fear, aggression or excitement. The intensity of the stimulus is then slowly increased incrementally until the puppy gets used to higher intensities, and eventually to

ABOVE *Always introduce new experiences such as grooming in a gentle and non-threatening manner.*

LEFT *The puppy learns to relax in the presence of unaccustomed sounds.*

the full intensity of the stimulus that initially evoked the inappropriate response. If, for instance, a puppy is fearful of certain noises, such as the vacuum cleaner, a sound CD could be made of the sounds in question, played at a very soft volume initially and gradually increased as long as the puppy does not revert to fearful behaviour. The volume should be increased very slowly, so that the original fear is not elicited.

Desensitization is used in conjunction with counterconditioning, which teaches the puppy a different emotional response to a specific stimulus. Instead of reacting with fear or aggression, the puppy is taught to relax. This process involves relaxation training (see Chapter 6). The puppy that is frightened of sounds would be taught to lie down quietly while the CD is playing, constantly rewarding it for calm behaviour. It would also be encouraged to play with a favourite toy, so that eventually the stimulus will become associated with positive things such as food and toys.

Desensitization and counterconditioning should take place regularly, preferably daily, for 10–20 minutes. Short, more frequent sessions are ideal. Depending on what the puppy is being desensitized to, it may take anything from days to months to produce positive results. The puppy should not be exposed to the full intensity stimulus during the process, as this will undo all the good achieved up to that point. During a session, if the puppy does revert to inappropriate behaviour, immediately withdraw the stimulus and reintroduce it at a lower intensity. Always end a session with the puppy relaxed and coping well.

Ensure that there are no physical problems

You should confirm that the cause of your puppy's wayward behaviour is not related to a physical problem that requires veterinary treatment. Let your vet examine the puppy and address any medical issues.

Troubleshooting

Some of the more common problems puppy owners encounter are listed here alphabetically and discussed briefly. Physical (medical) problems are discussed in Chapter 8.

Attention-seeking behaviour

Dogs are social animals and love attention from people, but when they become overdependent on attention they become a nuisance. Examples of attention-seeking behaviour are:

- Excessive barking, howling or whining
- Jumping up and pawing at people
- Mounting people and objects
- Mouthing people's hands and arms
- Grabbing objects and running off with them
- Maintained eye contact in order to elicit some form of social interaction

Puppies that show excessive attention-seeking behaviour have become unnaturally dependent on attention. To them, any is better than none at all, so even negative attention is reinforcing to them. Paradoxically, these puppies are usually already getting a lot of attention, often too much. They have learnt that whenever they ask for attention, they get it. The more they can get, the more they want, becoming anxious and inse-

cure when they think attention is no longer freely available. In a vicious cycle, this anxiety leads to even more attention-seeking behaviour.

To reduce the anxiety, interaction with the puppy must be controlled so that it learns that attention is not freely available whenever it wants it, but will be provided adequately on your terms. It must learn that attention and interaction can be earned by behaving calmly.

Do not inadvertently reinforce a puppy's attention-seeking behaviour by reacting to it. Do not respond to gratuitous pawing, jumping, vocalization and other behaviour that is designed to elicit a reaction from you. Ignore the puppy (look away, keep quiet, do not touch, turn your back – see Chapter 4) when it insists on attention. It is

143

LEFT *Door-scratching is an example of attention-seeking behaviour.*

always be initiated by you, and alternated with periods of no attention.

Be proactive about interacting with your puppy and more aware of how and when you interact with it. Even puppies that do not have attention-seeking problems will benefit from this approach. The nuisance puppy will calm down notably within a few days of adopting this strategy as the anxiety dissipates and it feels more secure. It is important though to follow through with this approach and not revert to a reactive attitude at a later stage.

Barking and whining

Puppies whine because they need something – they may be hungry, cold, lonely, or need to do their business. Manage excessive whining by first addressing all these needs.

However, if after you have addressed these needs the puppy still continues to whine for no apparent reason, you will have to pretend that you don't hear it, and pay attention to it only once it stops whining. This could mean it will go on and on – and that will require immense self-control on your part! However, if you are consistent in not responding to its whining, it will soon learn that keeping quiet has a better result than whining unnecessarily. It is usually necessary to endure persistent whining only two or three

not asking for affection, it is asking for feedback about who controls interaction and knowing that it's you makes it feel more secure. React when it behaves appropriately, i.e. not expecting or demanding attention but just quietly lying or sitting down, or playing with a toy. Interact on your terms, not the puppy's.

Ensure that it does get enough quality interaction by implementing a controlled interaction programme: Short, frequent interactions (for example, training for five minutes, playing a game, grooming it or going for a walk) should times before the puppy learns that it doesn't work, and behaves properly.

Puppies start to bark at about six months of age. Excessive barking could be caused by boredom, attention-seeking behaviour (at some point, it knows, you will come out and shout at it – better some interaction than none at all, from the dog's point of view) or social facilitation (the dog barks because other dogs bark).

Some breeds are particularly prone to nuisance barking. For example, most of the terriers, German Shepherd Dogs and some of the scent hounds fall into this group.

To address inappropriate barking, first ensure that you are not inadvertently reinforcing it by reacting to it. Secondly, make a point of rewarding appropriate behaviour – mark those quiet moments with tasty treats, or a click and a treat if you are clicker training. Your puppy probably spends more time being quiet than being a nuisance barker – you are just not noticing it. Thirdly, identify the possible reasons for barking and address them. Your puppy may need more exercise, more training, more quality time with you or more environmental enrichment to alleviate boredom. If there are specific triggers for barking, try to address or avoid these. And if the stimulus is unavoidable, the puppy must be desensitized to the cause of the barking.

RIGHT *A puppy that barks excessively may need more mental and physical stimulation.*

145

Begging

Many people complain bitterly about their dogs begging at the table. This is always a problem of our own making! We allow puppies to beg at the table and then reinforce the behaviour by feeding them titbits.

Right from the start, the rule should be that the puppy is ignored completely while people are eating. Ensure that it has a comfortable place to rest and some toys to occupy it, and then get on with your own meal. Do not respond to any whining, pawing or other attention-seeking behaviour – simply ignore it. Only once everyone is done and the table is cleared, does the puppy get attention again.

Encourage the puppy that has already learnt to beg, to settle down on its settle mat for 10 seconds while you pretend to be eating and slowly increase the time period. Persistent beggars may need to be confined in another room, or put into the indoor kennel or playpen while people are eating.

Biting (aggression)

Puppies often get overexcited during play and start chewing human flesh (see 'Play-biting', p154). If your puppy exhibits true aggression (uncommon in young dogs) characterised by growling, snarling, snapping and out-of-context biting, it needs to be addressed urgently as it could develop into a serious problem as the puppy grows older and stronger. Aggression is usually triggered because the puppy perceives a threat to its control over a resource (a bone, for example), or it is fearful, cannot escape from the cause of the fear and reacts defensively.

Aggression is often learnt behaviour. When a puppy feels trapped in a threatening situation, it may learn to react aggressively. Remember, you have control over what your puppy learns so ensure that it does not learn that aggression is a good option in difficult circumstances: Avoid

situations in which it may feel threatened with no option to escape.

Do not punish the puppy for aggression, as it will make the problem worse (it will justify its aggression). You should act neutrally if your puppy displays aggressive behaviour and remove it from the situation as calmly as possible and then avoid similar situations until you have been able to consult with a professional. Have the

ABOVE *Your puppy should willingly give up bones, chews and toys to you.*

puppy examined by a veterinarian, as a variety of physical conditions can be associated with inappropriate aggression in dogs. Aggression in young dogs is not appropriate and must be addressed immediately.

147

ABOVE *Encourage your puppy to sit calmly when people arrive at the door.*

Puppies with aggression problems should ideally be seen by a qualified animal behaviour therapist. Ask your vet for a referral. Treatment will include, amongst other things, desensitization and counterconditioning.

Boisterousness/excitability

A very boisterous puppy may cause injury to people and damage to property due to its inability to calm itself. A five-month-old large breed puppy is quite capable of knocking over a child or an elderly person, or accidentally dislodging the Ming vase from its pedestal.

Boisterous puppies need an outlet for their physical energy in the form of increased exercise and active play, but they also need to learn self-control. See Chapter 6 for self-control and relaxation exercises.

Identify and control the triggers for excitable behaviour, such as animated conversation, children playing or other dogs in the street. Anticipate situations that may excite the puppy

and occupy the puppy with another fun activity. Desensitize the puppy to triggers that cannot be controlled and reward the puppy whenever it is calm and relaxed. Use a lead if necessary to control the boisterous puppy.

Puppies that are excessively boisterous when their owners arrive at home often learn to behave like that because their owners unintentionally reinforce this excited behaviour. People tend to enthusiastically greet their dogs, with animated voices and lots of physical activity. This high level of excitement often gives rise to other problems, like dogs fighting with each other.

Keep the homecoming low key by ignoring your puppy when you arrive home – greet it only once it has calmed down. Look the other way, keep quiet and don't touch it (pretend it's not there) until it relaxes. This is the behaviour of a competent leader, which is what your puppy appreciates and needs. (See also 'Jumping to greet', p152.)

Chewing/destructive behaviour

Puppies are naturally investigative, and using the mouth and teeth is part of their exploratory behaviour. Teething occurs between four and six months of age and this seems to coincide with a particularly destructive phase for many puppies. You will need to manage your chewing puppy by not allowing it access to areas where it may cause damage to valuable or dangerous items. Keep chewable objects out of your puppy's reach, and make its own chew toys attractive

with peanut butter or cheese spread, for example. Have enough appropriate chew objects available and make them more attractive than anything else. Add value to toys by occasionally picking them up, handling them, even talking to them in an animated tone (you'll be forgiven for wanting to do this in private), especially when you need to redirect your puppy's attention from something else to a toy. Use baby gates or similar barriers to prevent access to forbidden areas.

Excessive destructive behaviour is not normal in puppies and could be the result of boredom

ABOVE *Don't let your armchair become your puppy's favourite chew toy.*

(lack of stimulation), anxiety (often separation anxiety – see below) or attention-seeking behaviour (this typically occurs in the owner's presence only). Ensure that the puppy has enough toys (rotated regularly) to entertain it, that it has lots of physical exercise and that it has adequate quality time with people.

Digging

Dogs dig because they are bored, to create a comfortable resting spot or simply because it's fun (digging is self-reinforcing). It is an instinctive behaviour – small terriers, for example, were bred to dig into the burrows of small mammals during hunting. Dogs may dig to bury items of high value such as bones.

Once a puppy has started digging, it is usually difficult to convince it that digging is not fun. Try to make the digging less enjoyable by placing chicken wire, corrugated iron sheeting or dog droppings just below the surface of the soil. If your puppy is digging for temperature regulation (to make a resting place), provide a sheltered alternative sleeping place, shady in a hot climate and warm in a cold climate.

If your puppy likes to dig a sleeping patch in different places, try to encourage digging in one spot only and make that spot available to it whenever it is outside on its own. Make other places in the garden less attractive and less accessible (with the temporary use of branches, chicken mesh or similar obstructions). Bury a rawhide bone (see Chapter 9) or something smelly in the designated digging patch to make it more attractive. You can even construct a proper sandpit on a bed of stone (for good drainage).

ABOVE *A certain amount of digging is normal for most dogs. Restrict your dog's digging to specific areas.*

Uninterested in training

See 'Testing teenagers', page 157.

Fears and phobias

The body language of a fearful puppy includes holding its body low, avoiding eye contact with the fear-eliciting stimulus or running away from it, tucking its tail between its legs and keeping the ears flattened. Sometimes the hair is raised (usually on the shoulders and at the tail base). A high-pitched bark or cry often accompanies fear. If the puppy cannot escape from the cause of its fear, it may become aggressive. Urinating and defecating, together with the other signs indicate the puppy is experiencing intense fear.

It is normal for puppies to be fearful of certain things though they often adapt to fear-eliciting stimuli over time and lose their fear. A puppy can develop a fear of just about anything, but the most common fears include strange people and loud noises. It is possible for a puppy to have multiple fears. A phobia is an intense, out-of-context fear reaction to a particular stimulus. Certain breeds, like Border Collies and some other herding breeds, tend to be sensitive and more likely to develop fears.

As puppy caregivers, we often feel sorry for a fearful puppy and console it when it is frightened. This unfortunately reinforces the fear, because the puppy perceives that being frightened gets a positive response. Be matter-of-fact when your puppy is fearful. Show by example that relaxed behaviour works in scary situations.

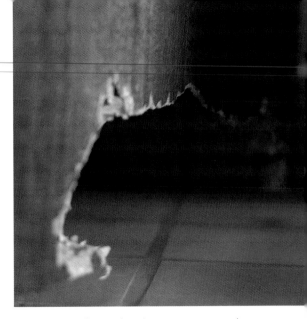

ABOVE *Intense fear and anxiety can cause severely destructive behaviour. This door was destroyed by a dog with an intense fear of thunderstorms.*

Puppies benefit from knowing that we are there when they are scared, but fussing over them at such times could make the problem worse.

A very effective approach towards fearful and phobic dogs is desensitization and counter-conditioning. In some cases, drugs that reduce anxiety may be indicated. These medications have to be prescribed by a veterinarian.

Grab-and-run

Grabbing items and running off with them is something puppies learn to do in order to initiate a chase game. By chasing the snatching puppy, you are simply reinforcing the behaviour. Put valuable items out of reach. When the puppy does grab something, walk away and pretend

you didn't notice. Pick it up later when the puppy has lost interest. Should you really need to retrieve the item, call the puppy to you in a friendly manner and exchange the item for a treat. This way you are teaching the puppy a valuable skill – dropping items from the mouth (see Chapter 6). You can also replace the dropped item with another, attractive chew or other toy instead of giving a treat. Use a long, trailing lead to control your highly motivated snatcher if it is too fast for you.

Jumping to greet

Persistent jumpers need very clear feedback about what works and what doesn't. They either do it because their jumping has been unintentionally reinforced in the past, or because they have an excessive need for attention and they have learnt that jumping gets them attention.

Deal with this problem in a planned training session, i.e. do not deal with it when it is really happening. When you arrive at home with your hands full of shopping and wearing your smart clothes, you will not be able to communicate clearly what you expect from the puppy. Try to avoid these situations temporarily until the puppy has learnt how to behave, and at first deal only with a situation staged specifically to train the puppy.

Put on old clothes and be ready with your interrupter such as a shake can (see Chapter 4) and a handful of treats. Try to recreate the situation as it normally occurs, i.e. come in through

ABOVE *Trade in a forbidden object for something more valuable like a treat.*

the same entrance. Observe the puppy very carefully and as it shows the intention to jump, turn sideways to foil the launch and shake the can near its head. Do not shout at the puppy or push it away. Then reinforce an alternative, non-compatible behaviour such as sitting. Two people can work together – one interrupting, the other doing the rewarding.

If you are doing clicker training, click when the puppy has four feet on the ground. Throw the treats on the ground. Keep clicking for 'four feet on the ground'. Reinforce with a jackpot if it sits or lies down instead of jumping.

Use a lead, with a head collar (Chapter 6) if necessary, to control the puppy if it is very excitable. Again you will need two people – one to hold the lead and control the puppy and one to be the 'victim' who can also reward it for good behaviour. Reward it for not jumping, but withhold all interaction if it does jump.

Ensure that the jumper gets enough physical exercise on a daily basis and that its social interactions with people are adequate and properly controlled. (See also 'Boisterousness', p148.)

Messing in the house

Young dogs that still mess in the house either never learnt properly where the appropriate locations for eliminating are, or are stressed by something and therefore start marking in the wrong places. (See also 'Urinating when greeting people', p161.) Rarely, there could be a physical abnormality of the urinary system. Ask your vet's help to rule out this possibility.

If the puppy has always messed in the house, i.e. there is no identifiable period during which it was clearly house-trained, the problem is probably due to a lack of learning. This puppy needs to be re-house-trained (see Chapter 3). Anticipate, observe and ensure that the puppy is in the appropriate location when it needs to go, and reward correct behaviour. The older a puppy becomes, the harder it is to do this successfully. If you are doing clicker training, wait for the instant it finishes before you click and treat.

ABOVE *Keep quiet, fold your arms and turn your back when the puppy jumps.*

153

The previously house-trained puppy that starts messing in the house usually has an underlying anxiety that needs to be addressed. This is often related to social relationships. There could be tension with another dog in the household, or insecurity due to a lack of competent human leadership. You may need the help of an animal behaviourist to address the underlying issue.

Play biting

Rough play often leads to biting. Here are some ideas to teach your puppy how to control its mouth (bite inhibition):

- The instant the puppy bites too hard (gentle mouthing can be allowed), stop the game. Keep your hand (or whatever is being bitten) still and use your other hand to redirect the puppy to an attractive toy. Make the toy more attractive by shaking it. Reward the puppy with praise and a controlled tug game when it takes the toy instead of your limb.

- Some puppies get so immersed in play-biting that they need something more notable to stop their playing. Interrupt the puppy with a loud noise such as a shake can, or even a loud, high-pitched screech (OUCH!). When the puppy lets go, withhold all interaction for a few minutes. Fold your arms; keep your feet still and out of reach if possible. You may need to close a door between you and the puppy to make it clear that you are no longer interested in interaction. The puppy must learn that play stops when biting starts. When you return, immediately start playing with a suitable toy and reward the puppy for appropriate play with praise, titbits or more (controlled) play. You may end up leaving and returning several times within a play session, but it is worthwhile to persist.

- Use a trailing lead, preferably with a head collar (Chapter 6) to control the puppy the instant it bites too hard. Every time it is successful with biting and is not stopped, it is in fact being reinforced for that behaviour and will be more likely to do it again in future. Redirect it to an appropriate toy.

ABOVE *Freeze the instant the puppy bites too hard. Redirect biting to a suitable toy.*

ABOVE *Puppies that nip at feet and ankles are reinforced by the movement of the feet. Freeze and redirect the puppy to an appropriate toy.*

Resistance to handling (the wriggling puppy)

Sometimes a puppy actively resists handling by wriggling vigorously, even resorting to biting the handler. These puppies need to be desensitized to handling. But there is no point in forcing an uncooperative puppy to be handled – the puppy will simply learn to resist more and more.

Start off by touching the puppy on the least sensitive part of the body, for example, on the chest. Avoid face, head, feet and flanks initially, and do not force the puppy on its back. Give it a good rub – massage the skin with your fingers. As you do this, observe the puppy carefully – if it remains relaxed and does not tense up, give it a treat every few seconds. Once it is comfortable with being touched in an area, move to another area. As long as it remains calm continue feeding it treats. Do this only for a minute or two and release the puppy while it is still relaxed. Repeat the exercise a few times every day, gradually extending the duration and the extent of handling. Move gradually along to the head, face and feet, continually feeding treats if it remains calm. At some point it will flop down on its side – at this point you may gently tickle its tummy.

If the puppy does tense up during one of these sessions, move your hand back to a more comfortable spot and wait for it to relax before you withdraw. Then, with the next session, slow down your approach even more.

155

ABOVE *Your puppy should allow handling all over its body without displaying any anxiety.*

When you can comfortably touch the puppy all over its body while it is lying down, introduce other handlers one by one, so that it gets used to being handled by different people. You can feed the treats while the other person is doing the handling. Although this process requires much patience, it is really worthwhile – an adult dog that is hand-shy or aggressive when handled, is far more difficult to treat than a puppy who is handling-resistant .

Separation-related problems

Puppies that are excessively destructive in their owner's absence may suffer from separation anxiety, which indicates an overdependence on the presence of the owner. However, all dogs that are destructive in their owner's absence do not necessarily suffer from separation anxiety. Active dogs that become bored when alone can also become excessively destructive.

Other symptoms of separation anxiety are excessive vocalization (barking and howling) and inappropriate elimination while the owner is absent (i.e. a house-trained puppy that messes only when left alone). Separation anxious dogs typically exhibit very exuberant greeting behaviour when the owner comes home and will not the leave the owner's side. Dogs with separation anxiety show signs of severe anxiety while alone, for example, pacing, hypersalivating (secreting excessive amounts of saliva) and hyperventilation (panting). These symptoms often start when they anticipate being left alone, for example, when they perceive signs of the owner leaving, like picking up the keys or the briefcase (departure cues).

Dogs that are simply overactive due to boredom do not show these signs. Bored, overactive dogs also do not show signs of destructiveness as consistently as dogs that are truly suffering from separation-anxiety.

Separation anxiety is uncommon in very young puppies; symptoms of the condition only usually start after six months of age.

Treatment for separation anxiety may require a combined approach of behavioural modification and medication. The puppy needs to learn to cope with being left alone, i.e. it must learn to react to solitude with relaxed behaviour rather than anxious behaviour. It also needs to learn to be more independent and not constantly in need of the owner's presence.

Relaxation training (see Chapter 6) involves teaching the puppy to lie down calmly for extended periods of time and with various distractions. Independence training involves leaving the puppy alone for gradually increasing time periods. It needs to first get used to staying alone for short periods while you are at home. You also need to desensitize it to your departure cues. This involves introducing departure cues at times when you are not about to leave, for example, picking up the keys when a departure is not imminent, so that the association between the departure cue and the actual departure is eventually broken.

During the implementation of the treatment, it is best not to leave the puppy alone for long periods. Puppy day care or a puppysitter may be necessary for the first few weeks.

Shyness

A puppy that is unwilling to approach a human and shies away from being handled can become very difficult to handle as an adult dog. Now is the time to rectify the problem. Do not force yourself on the puppy. Sit down on the floor

ABOVE *Don't fuss about the puppy when you are about to leave it alone.*

157

ABOVE *This seven-month-old Borzoi puppy is shy but not altogether unwilling to interact.*

treat gradually closer and closer to you to encourage the puppy to approach you. Let the puppy sniff you when it comes close enough. Do not make an effort to touch it until it is quite comfortable to be close to you. Maintain non-threatening body language – do not make direct eye contact, do not make sudden movements, keep yourself low, turn your head and/or body sideways. Once you can touch it, just do it briefly and then reward it. Refer also to 'Resistance to handling – the wriggling puppy' (p155). This process may take a few days or a few weeks before the puppy will voluntarily come to you for handling. Be very patient and let the puppy lead the pace of progress.

Social maturity

Dogs reach social maturity well after they reach sexual maturity. Whereas sexual maturity occurs at six to 10 months of age (later in some cases), social maturity is reached at 18–36 months of age. This is when dogs become aware of social status. Resource control can become an issue at this stage. This is seen more commonly in some of the guard and defence breeds as well as the terriers. The dog entering social maturity may become aggressive to other dogs and/or people. As a puppy owner you need to be aware that your puppy may become much more serious at social maturity, and less sociable. Any incident of aggression should be discussed with a professional behaviour therapist to prevent it from becoming a long-standing problem.

without moving and allow the puppy to approach you.

Clicker training works very well with these cases – with the tiniest step towards you, click and toss the puppy a treat. You can also just toss a treat if you don't do clicker training. Throw the

Testing teenagers

At around six months of age puppies naturally become more independent and more interested in their surroundings than in their caregiver. The terrible teenager, previously a perfect puppy, may suddenly lose all interest in training and ignore you completely.

You will need to stand firm and be more consistent than ever before. Do not feel that because you are no longer the centre of your adolescent puppy's universe, that it doesn't like you anymore and that you now need to spoil it. It is simply too comfortable with you and so interested in the world beyond you, that it forgets about you.

Remind it that you are the most important thing in its life by being the only source of nice things: It should not be able to get treats, food, toys, walks, games or anything nice in any other way than paying proper attention to you first. Insist on a 'sit' before feeding it. If it does not comply, put the food away and only feed again several hours later (provided it follows your instruction first). Pick up the food bowl consistently within 15 minutes (whether it has eaten or not). Hand out treats only if it has earned them by listening to you. No fun happens unless it does what you asked first. When you take very clear control of its resources, the teenager is reminded that you are indeed the ultimate provider, and will respect you as such.

Time-outs can be effective for adolescents with an attitude. If you start training and it

ABOVE *A time-out area should contain nothing of interest to the puppy.*

ignores you, enclose it in an uninteresting area for a few minutes. There should be nothing interesting at all for it to see or do, for example, an enclosed courtyard or the bathroom. Go out of sight, keep quiet and wait a few minutes. When you return, reward the first sign of interest it shows, even just a movement of the head towards you. Do the 'focus' exercise as described in Chapter 6. If it starts to ignore you again, leave immediately and repeat the exercise after a few minutes.

ABOVE *Lower yourself when greeting your puppy to reduce the likelihood of submissive urination.*

Once you have its focus, you can progress to other training exercises. Do not expect it to do complicated exercises. Keep the sessions short, fun and frequent. Remain calm – because if you get frustrated it will show in your body language and tone of voice and your puppy will become even less cooperative. This is a challenging phase, but you can take heart from the fact that it does eventually pass.

OPPOSITE *Always be consistent with your teenage dog. Insist on a sit-stay before you allow it to eat.*

Urinating when greeting people

Very young puppies have a poor ability to control their bladder muscles. They easily urinate involuntarily when aroused. If your puppy tends to make a puddle when you arrive at home, make less of a fuss at homecoming and maintain a low-key attitude (see also 'Boisterousness', p148). Do not interact at all with the puppy unless it has calmed down. Lower your body when you do greet it, so that it doesn't feel so threatened by your approach. Do not punish the puppy for messing inside – it did not do it on purpose. Most puppies outgrow submissive and excitement urination. A small number of puppies may need medication to help them control their urination urge more effectively.

8

Health

VISITING THE VETERINARIAN

Your vet will be your partner in caring for your puppy. A good relationship with a veterinary practice will help you give your puppy the best possible care. Your vet will come to know your puppy and all its problems intimately, and will be in the best position to advise you about matters affecting your puppy's well-being. Discuss the following important issues with your vet as soon as possible:

- Vaccinations
- Deworming
- External parasite control (fleas, ticks, lice)
- Worm control
- Congenital (present at birth) abnormalities

Make sure that you choose a vet with whom you feel comfortable. Do not be shy to ask questions about the services offered (which may include puppy training), such as fees charged, payment policy, emergency services and hours of business. Have an open, honest relationship with your vet – tell the vet if there is anything about your puppy's medical condition that you don't understand and if you have any concerns about the treatment your puppy is getting. Provide your vet with as many details as possible about your puppy's condition when it is sick, and ensure you follow the vet's instructions carefully.

Take your puppy to the vet often when it is only a few months old. Preferably, the first visit should be fun and not associated with injections or other potentially traumatic experiences. Introduce the puppy to the practice staff, let it have a look around the surgery and make it a positive experience by feeding treats and playing with a favourite toy. If possible, you can also have it lifted onto an examination table just for fun. This way, it will be less likely to be frightened of going to the vet.

Continue fun visits to the vet even when your puppy reaches maturity and beyond. Dogs that are relaxed while at the vet are easier to treat and handle (also in other similar situations such as grooming parlours and boarding kennels), and are less likely to experience unnecessary stress. A relaxed dog also makes the visit to the vet much more pleasant for the owner.

SIGNS OF ILLNESS

The first sign of illness in a puppy is a loss of appetite. It may also be listless and less enthusiastic about play. Other symptoms that may indicate a need for veterinary attention are:

- Diarrhoea for longer than a day.
- Blood in the stool.
- Blood in the urine.
- Vomiting blood.
- Coughing up blood.
- Persistent vomiting.
- Difficulty or inability in getting up.
- Limping.
- Difficulty breathing.
- Absence of stool.
- Difficulty passing a stool.
- Discolouration of the mucous membranes: the gums, tongue and conjunctiva (membranes around the eyes) should be a healthy deep pink colour and should be shiny and moist. In some dogs the gums are naturally pigmented, either partially or completely. A good example is the Chow Chow, whose gums and tongue are almost always a dark blueish colour.
- Abnormal body temperature: A puppy's normal body temperature is between 38 and 39 degrees Celsius.
- Dehydration: Lift up the skin on the puppy's back between your fingers and let go. If it remains raised (tented) for a few seconds, the puppy is dehydrated. If the skin immediately

returns to the normal position, it would indicate adequate hydration at the time.

- Seizures.

Diarrhoea and vomiting

Diarrhoea and vomiting are usually signs of
gastroenteritis (an inflammation of the stomach
and intestines). It is quite common for puppies to
show these symptoms. Gastroenteritis can be
caused by a worm infestation, eating things that
upset the stomach ('garbage disease'), viruses

and other organisms. Puppies like exploring with
their mouths and often swallow non-food items,
or food that has gone off, which can irritate their
intestines. Most puppies do not tolerate milk
and develop diarrhoea from ingesting milk.
Numerous viruses can cause gastroenteritis. The

ABOVE *Puppies that are vomiting should not be
allowed to drink water freely. Rather let them
lick ice cubes to quench their thirst.*

most serious gastro-intestinal viral infection is parvovirus, which causes a severe, bloody diarrhoea and continuous vomiting.

Treat diarrhoea by withholding food for 12–24 hours depending on age (12 hours for puppies under three months). Leave water freely available. After 12 hours, feed something bland – a mixture of rice, cooked chicken (no skin or bones), and cottage cheese or a special commercial intestinal diet. Feed a small meal every two to three hours, until it passes a firmer stool.

If your puppy vomits more than twice in an hour, take away food and water for six hours, and give a small amount of water and/or ice blocks every hour thereafter for six hours. Only if it has not vomited again in six hours, should you offer it something bland to eat.

Take your puppy to the vet if diarrhoea persists for longer than 24 hours, or if vomiting does not clear up within 12 hours. Go to the vet if the stool contains fresh blood or is black in colour (an indication of intestinal bleeding often caused by hookworms). If at any stage your puppy is very listless or disorientated, do not delay and go to the vet immediately.

Persistent vomiting (more than twice an hour in excess of three hours) requires immediate veterinary attention. Your puppy may dehydrate if it continues vomiting without appropriate fluid replacement. Vomiting in the absence of passing a stool may indicate an intestinal obstruction, which usually requires intensive treatment – this could include surgery.

Orthopaedic conditions

Puppies, because they are still growing, are quite susceptible to a variety of conditions affecting the bones and joints. Large and giant breeds are particularly susceptible to joint conditions, because they grow especially fast.

Elbow, shoulder and hip problems are well-known problems affecting large dogs. The most common conditions are hip dysplasia (HD) and elbow dysplasia (ED).

Hip dysplasia is an inherited deformity of the hip joint, which causes instability and resultant pain and discomfort. Elbow dysplasia is a cumulative name for a number of elbow abnormalities that affect young, growing dogs. HD and ED cause pronounced limping and difficulty in getting up. Although it is possible to diagnose these conditions in growing puppies, most dogs do not show symptoms until they are mature. Radiographs (X-rays) can confirm the presence of these conditions from 12 months onwards.

Hip and elbow dysplasia are inherited, but the manifestation of clinical signs depends to a significant degree on various environmental factors, in particular nutrition and exercise during the puppy's first year. For instance, diets too high in calcium and energy (especially during the first six months), and excessive weight-bearing exercise promote hip and elbow dysplasia.

These traits are inherited by complex genetic mechanisms, which make it difficult to predict the HD or ED status of puppies, based on the parents' status. The parents' genetic effect can

ABOVE *Hip dysplasia can affect dogs of different breeds and of all ages. It becomes particularly pronounced in older dogs, producing symptoms similar to osteoarthritis such as difficulty in getting up and lameness of the hind limbs. Although not common, puppies of 6 to 12 months can already show these signs.*

only really be determined in retrospect by establishing the status of a representative number of their offspring. Responsible breeding as well as careful management of puppies and young adults in terms of exercise and nutrition can curb the occurrence of hip and elbow dysplasia.

Some HD and ED cases can be managed with weight and exercise control alone while others may require chronic pain medication. More severe cases require surgery.

Neutering/spaying (sterilization, desexing)

Surgical removal of the reproductive organs is a common veterinary procedure. Castration refers to the surgical removal of a male dog's testicles, while spaying refers to removing the uterus and ovaries of the female. Neutering, sterilization and desexing are general terms encompassing both surgical procedures. These are performed mainly to prevent dogs from breeding (there is a worldwide overpopulation of dogs), and also in some cases to prevent or treat certain behavioural or medical conditions.

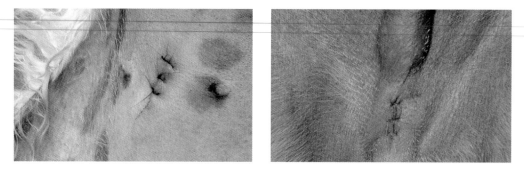

ABOVE *When a puppy of 4–6 months is spayed or castrated, only a small incision is required.*

Dogs reach puberty between six and 12 months of age. The female will show signs of heat (also known as coming into season) when it reaches sexual maturity. Signs of heat include a swelling of the vulva, a bloody vaginal discharge and interest from male dogs.

Intact (unneutered) male dogs may come from far and wide, and in large numbers, and could end up fighting amongst each other. The signs in the female continue for about three weeks. Initially, she will not allow the dog to mate with her, but about 10 days into the heat cycle she will stand for mating.

This is called oestrus and is the point at which the female is biologically ready to fall pregnant. During oestrus the bloody discharge and vulva swelling subsides. An unspayed bitch will come on heat every 6–10 months. A spayed bitch will not show any symptoms of heat and will not be able to have puppies.

The advantages of spaying a bitch are that she will not come on heat, will not have unwanted puppies and will be less likely to develop prob-lems related to the reproductive system, for example, pyometra (a uterine infection, often a fatal condition), cancer of the mammary glands and cancer of the uterus and ovaries. She will also be less likely to fight with other bitches (bitches in oestrus tend to be more aggressive).

Although the operation to spay a bitch requires abdominal surgery (hysterectomy) and general anaesthesia, it does not take long and does not usually require extended hospitaliza-tion. With modern drugs and surgical tech-niques, the risk of surgical complications is rela-tively low.

The advantages of castrating a male dog are that it will be less likely to roam (looking for bitches on heat) and fight with other male dogs, and mounting behaviour and urine marking will be reduced. Neutered male dogs are also not as likely to develop prostate problems. Neutering is a less complicated operation than the female spay, but does require general anaesthesia.

Neutering or spaying does not change a dog's personality. The procedure does not affect the dog's temperament in any way and it will not reduce its level of alertness or its ability to guard.

You should consider early on whether to have your puppy desexed or not. It is better to spay a bitch before she shows signs of coming into oestrus for the first time (bitches do not need to have puppies or go through a heat cycle before being spayed). Vets usually prefer not to spay a bitch while she is in season. Both male and female dogs can be neutered or spayed before they are six months old.

ADMINISTERING MEDICATION

It is very likely that during the course of your puppy's life, you will be required to give it medication. Always ensure that you clearly understand the instructions for use of any medication. Store your pet's medication (and your own!) well out of your puppy's reach.

To give a tablet or capsule, the easiest is to disguise it in something delicious like a piece of hot dog sausage (just big enough to swallow in one go). However, if your puppy does not have a good appetite or is not allowed to eat, you will have to administer it directly into the mouth. Open the mouth wide with your one hand pulling up the upper jaw and with the other hand, place the tablet right at the back of the tongue – it must feel like you are pushing your hand right down the puppy's throat. As soon as you have deposited the tablet and withdrawn your hand, close the mouth. It may help to blow lightly on the puppy's nose. Watch carefully – if

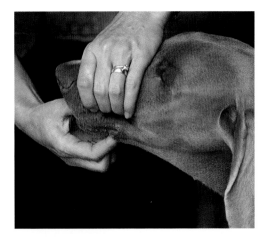

TOP and ABOVE *Using one hand to hold the upper jaw, open the lower jaw with the thumb of the other hand. In a calm manner and without hurting the puppy, put the tablet right down the puppy's throat.*

the puppy licks its lips, it means that it has swallowed. If it does not lick its lips, you will probably find the tablet on the floor a minute or so later. If you are unsure, open the mouth again and check whether the tablet is gone.

169

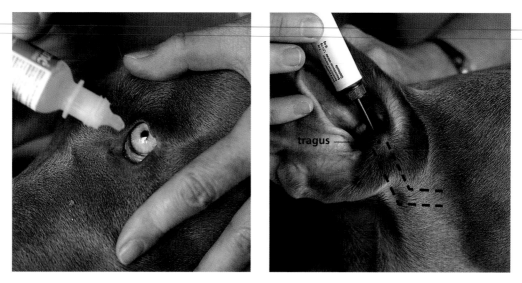

ABOVE LEFT *Pull down the lower eyelid to expose the pink conjunctiva.*

ABOVE RIGHT *Pull up the ear flap to expose the opening of the ear canal. The lines indicate the position of the ear canal.*

If you have to administer a fluid, you do not need to open the mouth at all. Use a syringe, lift the lip on one side and squirt the liquid in the little opening just behind the long canine tooth (eye tooth). Steady the head with your other hand to facilitate swallowing. Don't squirt too fast – give the puppy a chance to swallow.

To administer eye ointment or drops, ask someone to hold the puppy for you. Then, using the one hand, pull down the bottom eyelid, exposing the pink conjunctiva, and with the other hand, deposit the medication in the inner corner (canthus) of the eye (closest to the nose). It will automatically spread from there right across the eye. Wipe the tip of the tube before you treat the other eye so that you do not inadvertently trans-

fer an infection from the one eye to the other.

For ear medication, consider that the dog's ear canal consists of a vertical section first and then a horizontal part, before it meets with the ear drum which then leads to the middle and inner ear. You will only see the vertical section of the ear canal, and need to deposit the ear ointment or drops right at the bottom of the vertical canal, so that it can spread along the horizontal canal from there. Pull up the ear lobe, so that you can look straight down into the canal. If the puppy has a severe external otitis (ear inflammation), the space of the ear canal may be obliterated by the thickening of the ear mucosa. Look for the little projection of the ear in front of the earflap, nearer to the puppy's eye (the tragus, see picture

ABOVE *A healthy coat requires regular brushing and a high quality diet.*

opposite). This is your landmark – the tip of the tube must go in just behind this protuberance, down the vertical canal, in the direction of the corner of the jaw. Once you have the tube in place, squeeze and deposit the medication inside the ear. Wipe the tube after each ear. Rub the ear to facilitate the spread of the medication.

Coat care

Regular brushing gets rid of loose hair and dirt, massages the skin and helps the puppy to relax. Use a soft-bristled brush that won't scratch or hurt the puppy's skin. Even short-coated dogs need regular brushing. Regular bathing is not necessary, however.

You only need to bath your puppy if it has rolled in something dirty, or if it has a long coat that picks up dirt easily. It should not be necessary to bath a long-coated dog more than once a week. Frequent bathing may contribute to a dry, itchy skin. Use a shampoo recommended by your veterinarian. Long coats need daily brushing and should be groomed (cut) every four to six weeks. Wirehaired coats require less maintenance than long, silky coats.

A good quality diet with the correct combination of essential fatty acids contributes to a shiny, healthy coat.

9

Nutrition

WHAT TO FEED YOUR PUPPY

Commercial dog food manufacturers go to great lengths to do advanced research about the nutritional needs of dogs. They produce food from high quality raw materials in exactly the right balance to fulfil all the requirements of the growing puppy. You can use a home-cooked diet, but you have to be very careful that you do it correctly. For the growing puppy, controlling the calcium levels can be tricky with a home-cooked diet. High quality commercial dog foods provide everything in exactly the right quantities. The more expensive dog foods are generally the better ones, as they use better quality raw materials.

Dry (left) and wet (right) commercial puppy food.

DO NOT LEAVE FOOD FOR THE PUPPY TO NIBBLE ON DURING THE DAY

Firstly, it is more hygienic to feed separate meals. Ants, birds and household detergents may soil the food if it is left to stand.

Secondly, since one of the first signs of illness in a puppy is a loss of appetite you will not notice this as quickly when you leave its food out on a continuous basis. The sooner you detect a problem the better: those few hours could make the difference between a mild and serious medical condition.

Thirdly, and very importantly: Your puppy needs to recognise you as an effective resource controller (see Chapter 3 'Resource control and leadership'). Feeding meals is an essential part of controlling the food resource. If the food is always available, the puppy thinks that it controls the food resource ('whenever I am hungry I can go and eat'). If you feed meals and make it 'work' for its food, it will appreciate that you are the provider of the resource, will find it easier to trust you in controlling other resources for it too and will be more likely to listen to you and respect you. It will be more relaxed because it will not be stressed about resource control.

Dry pellets have more nutritional value per volume than wet (canned) food. You would need to feed a lot more wet food than dry food to obtain the same amount of nutritional value. Dry food is better for dental health than wet food, and it is cheaper. It is perfectly acceptable to feed your puppy only dry food. Moreover, puppies that are used to a dry diet are more easily cared for by other people when you leave your puppy in someone else's care while you are absent. However, wet food tends to be tastier than dry food, so puppies that are recuperating from an illness will do well on wet food and you can use it to encourage them to start eating again.

If you need to change your puppy's diet, ensure that you do it gradually. Sudden changes in diet could result in diarrhoea.

HOW OFTEN TO FEED A PUPPY

Puppies are first fed solid food from three to four weeks of age, four times a day. By the age of eight weeks, they can be fed three meals a day and from six months two meals a day. Feed specific meals – do not fill up the bowl once a day and leave the food out. Expect the puppy to carry out an instruction such as 'sit' before it is fed. Pick the food bowl up after 10–20 minutes. Puppies should only be fed if they are calm. Overexcited, uncontrolled behaviour should not be rewarded with food. Always ensure you have clean water freely available.

ABOVE *Food should not be freely available. Pick up the food bowl within 10–20 minutes.*

ABOVE *The nutritional needs of giant breeds (like the Irish Wolfhound) differ substantially from those of small breeds (Dachshund).*

Puppies have specific nutritional needs because they are growing, and are physically very active. Commercial puppy foods contain higher energy levels and high quality protein to assist with growth and physical activity. Mineral levels (for example, calcium and phosphorus) are also adapted for puppies, because the way that puppies metabolize minerals is different to how adults do it. Dogs should be fed puppy food until at least one year of age.

Different needs for different sizes

Large and giant breed puppies grow extremely fast, especially in the first six months. If they grow too fast and gain weight too rapidly, it makes them more susceptible to various orthopaedic problems (see Chapter 8). Larger breed puppies require less energy and lower calcium levels than smaller breeds. High energy and calcium levels will predispose them to hip and elbow dysplasia later on.

ABOVE *Puppies have different nutritional needs to adult dogs.*

ABOVE *Place an object such as a large stone in the food bowl if the puppy eats too fast.*

Calcium – not too much!

Before well-researched commercial dog food was available, dietary calcium deficiency was a problem with growing dogs (they developed rickets, a weakness of the bones). Nowadays, rickets is a very rare occurrence, and then only in dogs that are severely malnourished. It is indeed more common to see problems associated with excessive calcium intake (hip dysplasia and elbow dysplasia). Unlike adult dogs, puppies are unable to excrete excess calcium in the diet, and it is laid down in the bones where it causes bone weaknesses. Unfortunately, the concept of adding calcium to a puppy's diet has not died an easy death, and many people still want to add calcium to a puppy's diet when it is no longer necessary, and is indeed bad for the puppy's health. A good quality commercial diet has the correct calcium levels and will also take into consideration the size of the breed, as this affects the optimal calcium levels.

Fast eaters

Dogs are designed to eat fast, so if you have a vacuum cleaner puppy when it comes to mealtimes, it is probably normal. However, eating too fast can contribute to air swallowing which in turn causes increased flatulence. If you want to slow down your dog's rate of eating, put a large stone in its food bowl so that it has to eat around it, or put the pellets into a large flat container such as a tray. You could even feed the major part of the meal from a food-dispensing toy (such as a hollow cube for instance), so that it has to work harder for its food.

Slow eaters

Some dogs are slow eaters by nature. However, having a puppy that eats slowly is still not an excuse to leave food out ad lib. Twenty minutes is quite enough time for even a slow eater to finish its meal. Do not fuss over the puppy that picks at its food – this can become attention-seeking behaviour, with a puppy that will only eat if accompanied or even fed by hand. Be consistent and simply put down the food, march off and return within 20 minutes to pick up the bowl again (even if it hasn't touched its food). If you persist, at some point even the slowest eater will succumb and eat when the food is made available. Should your puppy suddenly lose its appetite, it is probably sick, so have it checked by the vet.

BELOW *Spread the food over a larger area such as a tray to slow down eating.*

OPPOSITE *Bones made from rawhide are a good substitute for real bones as they are less likely to cause dental injury.*

Bones

The feeding of bones to dogs is somewhat controversial: On the one hand, the dentists maintain that bones are harmful to teeth (and they can indeed cause tooth fractures and injury to the gums) and on the other hand, the behaviourists are of the opinion that the benefit of the mental well-being caused by the enjoyment of chewing bones, outweighs the dental risks. It is up to you to make up your own mind!

If you do feed bones, be very selective: Only large marrowbones should be given to dogs. Soup bones are too small for all but the tiniest of puppies. Raw bones are slightly better because they do not splinter as readily as cooked bones. Raw bones should be hygienic provided that they come from a reputable butcher. Ideally, the bones should have some meat attached to them as this will keep the puppy occupied for much longer. If a bone splinters into small pieces, remove it immediately so that the puppy cannot ingest pieces of bone; make sure you collect all the fragments and dispose of them.

Steak bones, chop bones, vertebrae, ribs and chicken bones are not suitable for dogs. These bones tend to fracture into small jagged pieces and can cause intestinal obstructions, which may necessitate extensive (and expensive) surgery.

Treats

Ensure that the treats you use for training are small, so that they do not interfere with the puppy's well-balanced diet. As long as the treats are small (pea sized), you can feed as many as you wish, but only if the puppy earned it through good behaviour.

No-no's

Most puppies are unable to digest milk sugar (lactose). This causes diarrhoea and resultant dehydration. Milk (other than mother's milk) is not a suitable food for puppies.

Chocolate and in particular dark chocolate, con-

tains theobromide and theophylline and can cause heart palpitations and nervous symptoms.

There have been some reports of raisins and grapes causing kidney failure in dogs. While this link has not yet been proven, it is wise to avoid these foodstuffs until definitive research provides more information.

Fatty, rich foods could cause gastroenteritis in puppies with sensitive stomachs.

ABOVE *Feed your puppy small, healthy treats when it deserves them.*

181

Glossary

Bite inhibition – a series of actions on the part of the trainer to control a puppy's mouth and deter it from excessive biting.

Capturing – a method of training where the puppy is placed in a situation in which the desired action is most likely; when the action occurs the puppy is rewarded .

Castration – removal of the male testes.

Clicker – a hand-held device that produces a sharp but neutral 'click' used to precisely mark a correct response by the puppy.

Counterconditioning – (see also desensitizing) teaching a dog to feel differently about a stimulus (changing emotion as opposed to changing behaviour).

Cue – a signal (either verbal or a hand movement) that is used to indicate to a puppy what it is required to do.

Default behaviour – the tendency a dog has, when it is unsure of what it has to do, to revert to how it was first taught to react in any given situation. For example, if it was taught as puppy to sit for treats, then the adult dog will tend to continue doing so.

Desensitizing (see also counterconditioning) – this is correctly referred to as systematic desensitization and describes a controlled process of gradual exposure to a negative stimulus (such as loud music, for instance) to get the puppy used to the stimulus. Initially, the stimulus is presented in its mildest form and then gradually and progressively intensified to a stage where the puppy is fully desentitized to it.

Desexing – surgical removal of the reproductive organs (see also neutering, spaying, castration).

Euthanasia – the act of putting any animal to death; veterinarians usually do this by injecting the animal with an overdose of anaesthetic.

Event and reward markers – the sound of the clicker; it means to the puppy that it did the right thing (event marker) and can expect a treat (reward marker).

Fear aggression – response by some puppies and dogs to a frightening stimulus; instead of fleeing, or if unable to do so, the animal will react with aggression.

Habituation – training to get the puppy used to its environment and things around it.

House-training – training a puppy to eliminate outdoors, preferably in a specific area.

Hypersalivation – excessive secretion of saliva.

Hyperventilation – panting.

Interruption devices – an implement that is used to interrupt a puppy's unwelcome behaviour; an interruption device can be as simple as a tin can with a few pebbles inside it. It is shaken vigorously at the moment the unwelcome behaviour takes place.

Luring – using something that is of value to the puppy – a toy, or a tasty titbit – to entice it to do voluntarily what the trainer wants it to do. The item being used is referred to as the lure.

Muzzle – a leather or nylon strap cage-like device that is strapped over a dog's muzzle to prevent it biting.

Neutering – general term applied to removal of male testes (or female ovaries).

Operant conditioning (also known as instrumental conditioning) – the process of learning through the consequences of one's actions – i.e. doing something either because it results in a positive consequence or because it avoids a negative consequence.

Paper training – the procedure that is used to teach a puppy that has to be left indoors for lengthy periods, to eliminate on paper.

Phobia – an intense out-of-context fear reaction to a particular stimulus.

Rawhide – a natural product made from cattle skin and used to manufacture imitation bones and chew toys.

Scent neutralizer – a solution or compound used to mask or counter the smell of urine or faeces.

Sociable behaviour – puppy is outgoing; readily interacts with humans, other dogs and animals. (Compare: submissive behaviour).

Socialization – exposure from an early age to pleasant social interactions with a variety of people, dogs and other animals to enhance appropriate social behaviour.

Spaying – removal of the female ovaries.

Stressor – anything within a puppy's immediate environment that is causing it undue stress and making it anxious; this could, for instance, be the sound of a vacuum cleaner, or even a dominant adult dog.

Submissive behaviour – a specific response in a social encounter, not necessarily related to fear, although it could be.

Substrate preference – the surface on which a puppy will come to prefer to eliminate; this may be the lawn, a paved area, an open area of bare soil, or – if the puppy has been paper trained – on paper.

Treat – a small titbit of food used to reward a correct response.

Trigger – something in its environment that causes a puppy to react, for instance a loud noise, return of the owner or the appearance of a cat.

Urine marking – the action by many animals, domestic and wild, to scent-mark their territory through marking the boundaries (by urinating on trees and lamp posts, for instance).

Further information on clicker training

Books

Alexander, M.C. *Click for Joy! Questions and Answers from Clicker Trainers and their Dogs* (2003). Waltham (USA): Sunshine Books Inc.

Aloff, Brenda. *Positive Reinforcement: Training Dogs in the Real World* (2001). Neptune City, New Jersey: T.F.H. Publications.

Pryor, Karen. *Clicker training for dogs* (2005). Waltham (USA): Sunshine Books Inc.

Videos

Clicker Clips. Kay Laurence, Learning About Dogs.

Clicker Clips Intermediate. Kay Laurence, Learning About Dogs.
PO Box 13, Chipping Campden, Glos. GL5 6WX, United Kingdom
www.learningaboutdogs.com

Clicker Training with Dr Quixi. EduPet.
PO Box 100689, Morelata Park, 0176 Pretoria, South Africa.
email: edupetmail@mweb.co.za
www.edupet.co.za

Puppy Kindergarten. The Clicker Training Center (Corally Burmaster).
www.clickertrain.com

The Art of Clicker Training with Karen Pryor. Waltham (USA): Sunshine Books Inc.

Websites

www.clickertraining.com
www.learningaboutdogs.com
www.clickersolutions.com

Toys and equipment

Treat-dispensing toys for dogs

www.bustercube.com
www.sitstay.com

Grooming brushes

www.companyofanimals.co.uk
www.puplife.com

Leads and harnesses

www.realdog.co.nz
www.petfooddirect.com

Associations

America

American Pet Association
PO Box 7172 Boulder, CO 80306-7172
tel: Main 800-APA-PETS (800-272-7387)
email: apa@apapets.org
www.apapets.com

Association of Pet Dog Trainers
PO Box 3734, Salinas, CA 93912-3734
tel: (408) 663 9257; 1(800) PET-DOGS
www.apdt.com

United Kingdom

Federation of Dog Trainers and Canine
  Behaviourists
15 Lightburne Avenue
Lytham St Annes, Lancs, FY8 1JE
email: gen@fdtcb.com
www.fdtcb.com

The Association of Pet Behaviour Counsellors
PO Box 46, Worcester, WR8 9YS
tel: (0) 1386 751151
email: apbc@petbcent.demon.co.uk
www.apbc.org.uk

Further reading

Coile, Dr Caroline. *Encyclopedia of Dog
  Breeds* (2005). Hauppauge, New York:
  Barron's Educational Series Inc.

Cunliffe, Juliette. *The Encyclopedia of Dog
  Breeds* (2005). Bath: Parragon.

Donaldson, Jean. *The Culture Clash* (1996).
  James & Kenneth Publishers.

Fogle, Dr B. *Dogalog* (2002). London: Dorling
  Kindersley Publishing.

Fogle, Dr B. *The New Encyclopedia of the
  Dog* (2000). London: Dorling Kindersley
  Publishing.

Pryor, Karen. *Don't Shoot the Dog! The New
  Art of Teaching and Training* (2002).
  Ringpress Books Ltd.

Index

Acknowledgements

Thank you to all the wonderful puppies and generous people who were our photographic models, to my staff members who worked extra hard to enable me to write, to friends, family and pets who patiently endured being ignored by me, to colleagues and clients for their support and understanding, and most of all to my husband and my daughter, Julius and Emma, to whom I dedicate this book with love.

With grateful thanks to our 'models' and their respective owners:

Moya, the German Shepherd, and Stefanie

Tauri, the German Shepherd, and Elizabeth

Rafferty, the Irish Wolfhound, and Brian

Lucy, the Irish Wolfhound, and Marcia

Molly, the Bulldog, and Anke and Anton

Lady, the Bulldog, and Anke and Anton

Milla, the Labrador Retriever, and Oomang

Juli, the Labrador Retriever, and Estelle

Jake, the Labrador Retriever, and Frik

Gina, the Standard Poodle, and Linda

Shasha, the Rhodesian Ridgeback cross, and Marianna

Obo, the Labrador Retriever and Clara, Denette and Therese

Mija, the Basenji and Francois

Vegas, the Afghan Hound, and Anne-matthi

Benji, the Dachshund, and Annalize

Libby, the Miniature Schnauzer, and Adrie

Max, the Weimaraner, and Annie

Tau, the Chow Chow, and Ronél

Oliver, the Miniature Dachshund, and Liz

Zinzan, the Dalmatian, and Willem

Ingrid and her menagerie: an adult Wire-haired Dachshund, an adult Doberman, an Irish Wolfhound puppy, and an adult Smooth-haired Dachshund

Monty, the Rhodesian Ridgeback, and Theo

Ella, the Rhodesian Ridgeback, and Theo

Bella, the Labrador Retriever and Gerhard

Fly Boy, the Afghan Hound, and James

Photographic acknowledgements

All photography by Ryno for New Holland Image Library (NHIL), with the exception of the following photographers and/or their agencies. Copyright rests with these individuals and/or their agencies:

Front cover, Gallo; p140, NHIL/Dorotheé von der Osten; p150, NHIL/Dorotheé von der Osten; p156, Robyn Steele; p167, Warren Photographic/Jane Burton; p168 Quixi Sonntag.